CONSCIOUS MASTERY

Also By Astara Teal Summers

Expand with Love ~ *A Guide to Recognizing Love in the Midst of Change*

CONSCIOUS MASTERY

FREEDOM FROM THE INSIDE OUT

ASTARA TEAL SUMMERS

BALBOA.
PRESS

A DIVISION OF HAY HOUSE

Balboa Press books may be ordered through booksellers or by contacting:

Balboa Press
A Division of Hay House
1663 Liberty Drive
Bloomington, IN 47403
www.balboapress.com
1-(877) 407-4847

Because of the dynamic nature of the Internet, any web addresses or links contained in this book may have changed since publication and may no longer be valid. The views expressed in this work are solely those of the author and do not necessarily reflect the views of the publisher, and the publisher hereby disclaims any responsibility for them.

The author of this book does not dispense medical advice or prescribe the use of any technique as a form of treatment for physical, emotional, or medical problems without the advice of a physician, either directly or indirectly. The intent of the author is only to offer information of a general nature to help you in your quest for emotional and spiritual well-being. In the event you use any of the information in this book for yourself, which is your constitutional right, the author and the publisher assume no responsibility for your actions.

Editor: David Lombardino & Associates

ISBN: 978-1-4525-3627-9 (e)
ISBN: 978-1-4525-3625-5 (sc)
ISBN: 978-1-4525-3626-2 (hc)

Library of Congress Control Number: 2011911191

Printed in the United States of America

Balboa Press rev. date: 7/5/2011

To my husband Freehawk and son Zachariah, whose love and support is an inspiration unto itself.

To my parents, who taught me more than they know.

There is only one time when it is essential to awaken:
That time is now ~ Buddha

CONTENTS

List of Illustrations:

Chapter 2 - Three Circles
Chapter 4 - Five Circles
Chapter 5 - Flower
Chapter 6 - Six Circles
Chapter 7 - Happiness
Chapter 8 - Fire
Chapter 9 - Warm Heart
Chapter 14 - New Life

FOREWORD

"A truly impressive book. Each paragraph is a treasure trove of insight worthy of deep contemplation. Filled with practical exercises and suggestions, Conscious Mastery facilitated my return to a place of mindful introspection and honoring of myself. Conscious Mastery is a powerful tool on the journey of spiritual growth and a must read for anyone committed to the path."

Scott Silverston, Author
Voices of the Earth, An Oracle of the Web of Life

ACKNOWLEDGMENTS

I would like to acknowledge and thank Samantha Bachechi owner of www.CreativeMedium.net for the initial creation of the star and background color for Conscious Mastery®.

I would like to acknowledge and thank Ty Andrews owner of www.ThinkupCreative.com for taking the initial creation to the next level to develop the look and feel of the business cards and book cover design of ConsciousMastery.org.

I would like to acknowledge and thank Bob O'Lary for the author photographs. His expertise and fun spirit made the process a real joy. Bob O'Lary Photography-Tallahassee, Fl.

INTRODUCTION

This book is dedicated to the transformational clearing and healing of the emotional body; an awareness and acceptance of our Divine Spirit and Divine Will; embracing the authentic self; and a true, deep, personal reunion with Mother/Father God. Transformation and healing, one and the same, illuminate and restore our intimate connection with Source and remind us of our own divinity. The understandings received on this path strengthen your desire and ability to be responsible for your overall health, wholeness, and happiness.

There are many different ways we can open to the endless supply of love from Source. The spark that ignited the path of change, opened my heart, and took me on a journey with no end came through song. More specifically, it was the awakened desire to sing. As the music and lyrics came through me, I strained to sing with all my heart, only to find my voice was buried beneath the burdens of life I unwittingly carried. My mind expanded, my emotions stirred, and my heart began to open. The process of finding my true voice began. The creative energy of song flowing through me brought understanding, transformation, and healing. After many years, the spark of change grew to become a flame of passion, which in turn cleared the ground of my heart to yield the new life of this book.

A desire to move toward unconditional self-acceptance and the unconditional love of all parts of ourselves is essential. In the beginning this may be challenging, yet with patience and perseverance, the journey becomes one of Grace. A connection or willingness to connect with God, Goddess, Divine Mother, Creator, Source, or whatever is deemed a higher power to be is imperative for those reading this book. It is in this connection that we find the guidance that will aid us in the restoration of the lost alignment of our Will with Divine Will and our Spirit with Divine Spiritual Consciousness. When our Will and our Spirit find balance in the Heart, we discover our internal guidance system and realize there is nothing we cannot do. Alignment with Source encourages balance between our Spirit and Will and our Heart. Through this balance, our internal guidance system guides us to the right place at the right time with the ability to execute right action.

I was told to tell my readers how easy it all is and how quickly everything will change. The truth is that it can be relatively easy and quick, if there is no resistance. However, for many of us it takes some time. It took time to develop patterns of behavior that lead to illness and unhappiness. So if it takes us some time and it is not all that easy, we should not worry or think we are the only ones that find evolving a challenge. Remember, we are learning to create consciously. Once this is understood and put into practice, we will have created a foundation of strength and courage with enough love to walk through any experience with grace and ease, trust and faith.

I am calling for us to face ourselves honestly and deeply, with as much love as we are able. This journey of self-discovery will have us dancing with our shadows, and then feeling our way back into the light. As many have come to know, our emotions are a vital part of our whole being. Our emotions have something to teach us. As we evolve and clear our emotional body, we come to know that our minds can no longer tell our emotions how to feel. Honest feelings are essential to our evolution. Through self-acceptance and the evolution of our emotions, our thoughts evolve too. When one thing is affected, it has an affect on everything else. The need for our mind to dictate how our emotions should be feeling is no more.

For those that come to read this book, I wish you a journey filled with Grace and love. Keep in mind we all have everything we need within us to evolve and heal ourselves. It is my hope that we will discover all the treasures that lie within us. All I ask is that we feel things for ourselves, and in the process, we will discover more of who we are and what makes our lives what they are. When we begin to see how we create our world, we can begin to create more of what we truly desire.

I do believe in miracles. I have experienced many miracles of transformation and healing in my lifetime. Like so many things that once seemed impossible, healing and transformation is possible for everyone. If there is openness and willingness anything can happen for anyone. What I share here comes by way of experience. It is my experience that patterns of behavior can and do break, providing energy for a new way of life. We are amazing creators when we create consciously.

The time is now to evolve our Spirit and our Will, represented by our thoughts and our feelings. We must bring ourselves back together and become whole once again. Do not worry about learning it all or knowing it all. The learning never ends and we will never know it all. It is not a concern to be better than or faster than someone else on this journey. This is a personal journey, unique and special. Be present. We evolve at a pace that is right for us individually. Let life unfold. This is a journey with no end to the learning, no end to the knowing, and no end to the process of evolving. All we really have to do is, get started. One step at a time always takes us somewhere. Where are you going? Where do you want to go?

Now we begin.

HOW TO USE THIS BOOK

Conscious Mastery: Freedom from the Inside Out, offers a complete multimedia experience, making this "more than just a book." The online Bonus Media Center includes links to guided audio meditations, PDF worksheets, and helpful videos.

As you go through the book you will see pages from my meditation coloring-book. I encourage you to get out your colored pencils and color right in the book. Each picture has a word or phrase on the page for you to meditate upon as you color the pictures. It is a creative way to bring thoughts and feelings to the surface. Let the energy move and to the best of your ability gently bring your mind back to meditate upon the word or phrase. From the Bonus Media Center you can download a larger version of each picture along with a short meditation to inspire positive change.

Few of us are fortunate enough to live surrounded by spiritual teachers and worldly philosophers, so we turn to books. The goal is not to collect information, but to gain understanding. So how do you know if you are on the right path? A good sign is when what you read forces you to stop, contemplate, and reread.

There comes a time when direct experience becomes the path and the answer. All the experiences we have had and will have are for the growth and expansion of our souls. It is my hope that we come to trust in ourselves and reconnect with Source in a way that is personal and meaningful to each of us.

To receive the Bonus Media register at
www.ConsciousMastery.org/BonusMedia

CHAPTER ONE

My Story

My story begins in Wisconsin in the mid-1950s. Much of my early years were painful, frightening, and unstable. As a little girl, I loved my parents deeply and in their own way I know they loved me too. With intent to heal and understand my life and myself, I grew to realize they did the best they could. I also realize they were both, in their own way, teachers of great value.

By the time I ventured out on my own, I had no life skills. And though it did not show on the outside yet, I was afraid of everything. In spite of or because of that I ran fast, with eyes closed, and no direction in mind other than to get as far away as possible. It did not take long before I found myself lying in a hospital bed, looking out the window at a brick wall. What a perfectly sad representation of my unconscious creation.

It was the Fourth of July 1974, my boyfriend at the time, I will call him Sam, and I had lied to my father. We had told him that Sam had his motorcycle license so we could take his bike out for a drive in the country. Somewhere along the way, I convinced Sam to let me drive. He put me in the driver's seat, put the face guard on my helmet (for which I am forever grateful) and with no instruction to speak of, away we went. The first sharp turn in the road scared me. I looked in the rear view mirror only to see Sam, my ostensible driving instructor, paying no attention to what I was doing. I had not been instructed on where the brakes were nor had I even thought to ask. In a panic, I pulled back on the throttle as if it were a brake on a bicycle. We accelerated, flew off the road, and straight through a barbwire fence. The fence first hit the face guard at eye level, then scraped down to the end of the face guard and broke when it hit my mouth, cutting my lip in half, knocking out my front teeth, cutting through the lower chin area of my face, and severing the nerves.

The next thing I remember, I was in a field shocked, dazed, and could hear a faint voice in the distance. It was Sam yelling at me to help him get the bike up and on the road. I entered a time warp and though it was late afternoon, I saw the sunrise. Memories of childhood fantasies getting in a terrible accident causing Mommy and Daddy to rush to my side, showering me with love and attention flowed through my mind. I knew in that instant I had created this. Fortunately for me, my soul had enough influence to apply a protection clause, thank God, because I always ended my fantasy with "I am alright in the end." I was five and six years old at the time of those creations and, of course, I had grown to forget I had thoughts like that. Still, here I was at 18, experiencing a terrible accident but the twist was Mommy and Daddy did not shower me with love and attention.

The doctor told me my lip would droop due to the severed nerves. He said nerves do not repair themselves and that I should expect no feeling in that area of my face. He was preparing me for the most hideous outcome. It was a surreal period of time. When I returned home to rest and repair, I had bandages across my face that my cat pounced on at any opportunity. I began to put my hands over my damaged face while praying for and thinking about healing my physical wounds. This is when I discovered the healing energy in my hands.

After a few months, I was able to begin the dental work and then had reconstructive surgery on my face five months later. The surgeon was surprised to know my scars were only five months old and said it looked more like five years. I continued with the healing hands after that surgery. One day I felt a hot flash run through my face. I knew it was a nerve finding a path. Today I have full feeling in my face and my lip never did droop.

Thinking about how I created this terrible experience led me to the book *The Power of Positive Thinking* by Dr. Norman Vincent Peale. Seeing the depth of my negative, self-destructive thinking patterns ignited a desire for change. I dove into the Bible, reading Proverbs over and over. I got excited when I remembered my childhood dream of wanting to sing, only to discover my voice was buried beneath layers of fear, grief, self-loathing, and denial.

Healing my physical body led to healing my emotional body, as I turned inward in search of my voice. I believed this was my ticket to freedom. Yes, I was going to be a rock star, make a ton of money, and all my troubles would be over. Strangely enough, it was my ticket to freedom, but in a way I had not considered or expected.

The initial awakening occurring at the time of the accident did not result in a straight and narrow path to healing. My wounded self was far too twisted, and I did not know what to do with the information I received. I stumbled along, made progress, fell down, got back up, and on it went. I know the saving grace for me was the reconnection I made with Source and my ongoing prayers for help. The patterns of self-hatred and self-destruction were deep and strong. Nothing was easy. I fell in and out of drug addiction, bad relationships, loneliness, and through it all, I wrote songs.

Unwilling to give up and finally willing to live, I dove deeper inward until I discovered a tiny spark of believing in myself. My ticket to freedom from a lonely confusing, painful, life came from the inside out. My connection with Source grew stronger bit by bit. In time, songs with hopeful and meaningful lyrics began to replace the songs I wrote of heartbreak and pain. This wave of music brought messages to assist me in understanding the power of thought and spoken word, forgiveness, the endless flow of love, and the importance of making room within for love to flow through me. This led me to recognizing and releasing my denial, guilt, judgment, and fear. Any day that brought me the awareness of something more to let go of, I did it. I learned how to speak my truth, express myself honestly, and with practice I was able to embrace discernment and speak my truth with love and kindness (most of the time). The messages I sang over and over sunk in to the measure of increasing my personal power to make conscious choices, stand up for myself, and shift my behavior. The desire to live life fully gave me the strength to put into action what I had learned.

This is a snapshot of my story. I did not know where this journey would take me, but I did know I was beginning to see the light and that in itself was an answer to my prayers. I was told my face would be deformed due to nerve damage, but it is not. I was told I had a speech impediment and was tone deaf, but today I can sing. I was told I could never write songs unless I learned other people's songs first, but I did. My artistic nature was never supported until I supported it. As soon as I gave myself permission to express the artist within, I began to create in many different ways. All the time we spend discovering and expressing our true nature through the avenue of creativity, whatever it may be, strengthens our connection with Source, whose love and support never ends.

When I began my journey, I had no road map. I endured extended periods of isolation. I do not recommend that, although I do recommend some healthy alone time. From tragedy, I renewed my personal communion with Source and the desire to find my true voice. We do not have to wait until something devastates us before we begin to change and experience a will to grow and live the life we desire.

The power of love created an opening, which led me to find valuable information in the many books I read and studied. The power of love led me to some wonderful, loving facilitators and teachers along the way. I have had teachers that taught me what to do and teachers that taught me what not to do. Both were of great value.

I never thought I would write a book until I was guided to write *Conscious Mastery*. No one told me how to do it; I followed my internal guidance and just got started. Getting started is an important key to creating change consciously. Life unfolds in interesting and magical ways that support our new growth. At the time I began the process of writing *Conscious Mastery*, I came across a TED video with the author Elizabeth Gilbert after she wrote *Eat, Pray, Love*. To paraphrase, she said, I just had to show up. I took that to heart and showed up every day to write. I persevered with the hope that *Conscious Mastery* may quicken the process of evolution for others by sharing what I learned after a lot of trial and error. We never know what we can accomplish until we set ourselves on a path of being who we have always been. Who we have always been is a powerful, creative being of great love. We are asked to participate in creating our lives and for that to happen, we have to show up.

Do not underestimate what you have to offer the world. There is a treasure within you, waiting patiently to be discovered, embraced, and cultivated. Shine your Light. Share your Gifts. Expand with Love. Feel what is real and allow the light to illuminate your path and your consciousness. The time is now to Live Life Whole, Happy, and Free!

New Beginning

CHAPTER TWO

WHEN THE ALARM SOUNDS

There are waves of energy touching everyone. Every person has his/her own internal alarm. When it goes off, the awakening begins. There is a subtle and sometimes not-to-subtle tug at the heart. Questions like, "Who am I? What am I doing with my life? What does this all mean?" begin to float into the forefront of the mind. There are those who have come before us in the awakening process and there are those who will awaken after us. Each person who hears the alarm and awakens has a choice. One choice is to ignore the alarm and fall back to sleep. The other choice is to stay awake and begin the journey of self-discovery. To dive deep within to find answers is the brave and wise choice indeed.

Some of the factors linked to our ability to awaken are related to our ability to receive new information. If we are in a heavy state of denial, it may take something very big to get our attention. Our receptivity to the Divine impulse of higher learning and awareness is related to our personal level of self-acceptance and healthy self-love. When unconditional acceptance is embraced in the light of ever expanding truth, an opening for new information, insights, and new perspectives is created.

Through denial, judgments, and all manner of suppressing the natural flow of energy we can be filled with old charge, which is made of repressed emotions, shadows, or inner demons. When we are heavy with denial, we are no longer available for new higher thought forms or information. We are simply not able to receive new information. We hear people say, "It's like I am talking to a brick wall." Sadly, many people have mastered the path of denial. Denied emotions and judgments must be recognized, accepted, and released before any new awareness or information can be received. Divine guidance is lost to us when we are steeped in the darkness of denial, our minds limited by judgment, and devoid of peace. This can change. No one is asked to release everything at once. Everyone, on some level, is being asked to either continue on their path to the light or to simply begin.

The Spirit and the Will together manifest in the body. If the Spirit's attempt to awaken us with flashes of insight is not accepted then the magnetic nature of the Will draws an experience from outer reality into our lives to get our attention. We all meet our vibrational match. If the experience can be seen for the opportunity it is, we can clear old charge and become receptive once again to new information. We are then on the path of gaining understanding. A noticeable shift in perception takes place because, little by little, we have broadened and illuminated our consciousness. The old paradigm of change, seen as bad luck or worse, needs to change so we can recognize these experiences as opportunities for growth, prompting us to create positive changes in our life with grace.

As always, we have a choice. We may choose to deny the reflection brought on by an experience designed to awaken us. If we opt for old, familiar behavior, such as blame and judgment, it will only serve to deepen and prolong the suffering brought about by squelching undesirable emotions. Avoiding the responsibility of being creators of our own lives does not change the fact that we are creators of our lives. To choose the old way is to remain asleep. To awaken is to explore all the possibilities with the intention of understanding ourselves, our lives, and reconnecting with Source. One choice reflects readiness to evolve; the other does not. This is not good or bad. Some are ready to expand and grow and others are not. Resist the urge to judge those who are not ready. Let go of the notion that we know what is best for others. Rather, we must allow them their right to choose and if their choice is too disruptive for us and our lives, we can walk away. There is no benefit in pushing or attempting to force someone to see what they cannot or are not ready to see. We can love them from a distance if we must, but still love them.

To give unconditional acceptance for everyone to live the life of their choosing does not mean we have to bring their choices into our lives if it does not feel good. It means we give them the space to grow or not grow in their own way and in their own time. Offering a helping hand or heart-felt suggestions is good, but if they choose not to embrace our goodwill, let go and move on. Chances are there is much to do within our own beings. Time is always well spent when we learn and embrace more of who we truly are. This is a journey with no end. There is always something new to learn and apply in our everyday life. In this way, we master levels of growth and prepare the soil for the next level of growth and change.

Go To Bonus Media Center at:
http://www.ConsciousMastery.org/BonusMedia
To Download Bonus Media for Chapter Two

CHAPTER THREE

WHAT OUR BELIEFS REFLECT

"Peace comes from within. Do not seek it without." Buddha

Here is a simple truth: whatsoever we believe is true for us. What we hold as a belief, whether we are conscious of it or not, plays out in our lives with great accuracy. Our outer world is a reflection of our inner world. Become curious enough to discover what belief systems you are embracing consciously or unconsciously. They can be seen in the dance of our ordinary days. Are our belief systems supporting us or weakening us? Do our beliefs promote a sense of unity or separation? Are our belief systems filling us with love or fear, hope or despair? When we begin to realize that the patterns playing out in our realities all reflect our belief systems, we become aware enough to begin making changes consciously. Is life reflecting a grand adventure filled with hope and abundance? Is life difficult and painful? Do we feel worthy of great love? Are we just making it through each day? Do our bodies reflect health or illness? Allow the truth to unfold. Wherever we find great resistance, there is a message. Move into this resistance gently, slowly asking for the nature of the resistance to reveal itself. Behind the wall of resistance, truth is waiting to speak. Listen for your inner voice and let go of resistance. It is time to flow toward happiness and the life we desire. We can do this one thought and one step at a time.

Life, Is It Simple or Complicated?

We have been taught to complicate matters and the more we complicate our lives, the more complicated and confusing our lives become. Conversely, the more we simplify our lives, the more we discover simplicity is Divine and a key to our evolution. The simpler we live, the more grace and goodness can be seen and felt every day. Truth is simple, pure, and uncomplicated. When truth is twisted and altered to serve some ulterior motive, it creates complications and confusion.

Being simple is not being a simpleton, foolish and gullible. Simple is a pure, unaltered, grounded way of living, easily done and easily understood. Simple is fundamental, straightforward, and uncomplicated in nature. Do our lives reflect a level of simplicity in all areas? It may be time to take a closer look into the areas of life that feel complicated and see what makes them so.

A complicated lifestyle has its own set of distractions. We may discover old and unproductive patterns of behavior as well as old belief systems hidden at the core of the complexity. This awareness may lend itself to sorting out and letting go of belief systems that keep us spinning in the same unsatisfying way. A return to the basics may open new possibilities and new ways of seeing and relating in many or all areas of life. When was the last time we completely unplugged and took a walk in nature or sat quietly bringing our attention to our breath? This is a simple thing we can do at any time. Becoming clearly aware of the need and desire for change does not necessarily call for drastic action but it does call for action. Make one move toward a better way of thinking. The next step will come and when it does, take it.

Exercise: Create a Road Map

Go to the Bonus Media Center to download- Creating My Road Map.

If you would prefer to create your own, here are the guidelines: Make a list of each day of the week; under each day give a brief overview of what you see and how you feel about what you are aware of. Give yourself room to write. It is a snapshot of what got your attention, both in awareness and in feeling. Next give a brief action step you took or could take, if it applies. It strengthens personal power to know there are solutions available for what does not feel good. It also strengthens personal power to provide a kindness that will lift someone's day and to recognize and acknowledge the kindness of others offered to you.

Here are examples:
What you see: I see my family all off in their own world.
What you feel: I feel isolated when no one communicates OR I feel free to do my own thing.
Action: I will take the first step in reaching out and spending some time with my children or spouse. OR I will read a good book or start that art project I have wanted to begin.

What you see: I see the unhappy store clerk.
What you feel: I feel ignored, as she will not make eye contact. OR I feel sorry for her obvious unhappiness.
Action: I did nothing, but wish I did. OR I wished her a good day.

What you see: I see chores piling up.
What you feel: I feel angry to be the only one responsible. OR I feel grateful to have help or be healthy enough to do them.
Action: I will ask for assistance or delegate some of the chores. OR I do them happily, knowing I can and so it is easy.

What you see: I see my coworkers.
What you feel: I feel agitated OR I feel happy to come to work because we are friends
Action: I will bring flowers to put on my desk to remind me of my garden. OR I will let my coworkers know I appreciate them.

You will discover more about your environment and more about you. You will see things that need more of your attention and many things to be grateful for. You will discover there are things that have had your time and attention that provide nothing in return. You will see your overall mind-set and attitude, in and out of the home. You will discover how you can brighten someone's day rather than let them pull you down. You will discover ways to brighten your own day and grow in self-reliance. You will discover there are things you really do not like and you do not have to continue participating in the same old way or at all.

Create a road map and you will begin to see more and feel more. Your beliefs will be reflected back to you. You will begin to make decisions consciously. It is a simple exercise but it is about taking action in becoming more aware of your life and making changes. One step at a time will take you somewhere. By becoming more aware of what you see and how you feel, you can decide in what direction you will take your next step.

"For those who believe, no proof is necessary. For those who don't believe, no proof is possible." Stuart Chase

Go To Bonus Media Center at:
http://www.ConsciousMastery.org/BonusMedia
To Download Bonus Media for Chapter Three

Balance of the Masculine/Feminine

CHAPTER FOUR

OUR SOUL AND THE DIVINE MOTHER

There is a lot of talk about the re-emergence of the goddess. Who is she and where has she been? She is intuitive, feeling and sensing emotion. She is soul aligned with experience and, when accepted, she is soul-full. She brings forth life into manifest reality. She is fertile, productive, and gives birth to life, projects, and ideas. Her energy is magnetic, Yin in nature, the negative polarity and is associated with Earth. She is the giver and the power of the Divine Mother. She is the Will. The correlation between the broken, denied, and fragmented Will and how we have mistreated and suppressed the goddess/Divine Mother along with all of her beautiful and powerful attributes is worthy of contemplation.

A free Will has the magnetic power to bring desires into manifest reality in a loving and kind manner. The emotional body is magnetic. The Will is magnetic. Desire is the magnetic energy of the Will that attracts the light; the essence of the light of God is love. The increased vibration of the magnetic polarity opens space for the essence of spirit, which powers creation. When our magnetic energy is compromised, our spiritual essence is diminished, therefore we lose light. In a sense, we become heavy and blind to the truth. The body is the expression of both the feminine yin (negative polarity) and the masculine yang (positive polarity). Both are vital to the whole of creation. The Will experiences and the Spirit illuminates consciousness. When we are clear, aligned with Source, and true to heart, Spirit and Will are in balance in the heart, expressing inspiration, feelings, and participating in the selection process of highest and best choices, guidance and action. The inner masculine and inner feminine complement one another. The Will is powerful and when someone has lost their will to live, they die. It may be a metaphorical death before the body gives way and the Spirit takes flight but with no Will, there is no life. The time is now to set our souls free.

The power of the Will is the power of the Feminine and it has struck fear in Man to such an extent and for so long that breaking the Will and suppressing the feminine has become common place. Learned helplessness is just one expression of wounded or broken Will. It is only through stories that the reign and power of the feminine exists at all. The fear of the feminine is evident throughout history, especially in the religious and political sectors but it is by no means limited to these areas. It is seen in family dynamics, the work environment, and in just about every place people gather. Free expression of feelings and thoughts was forbidden and all things feminine, such as intuition, deep wisdom, connection with the earth and the healing arts, were considered dangerous. Sadly we still see that today. The stifling and suffocation of the feminine has gone as far as it can without eliminating the human race.

Turning Point

A turning point occurred and women began to rise up. Many of the front-runners were stopped dead in their tracks, cut short of exercising their right to be. However, they blazed a trail through the jungle and I am forever grateful for their courage and their heart. Those in the front got the worst of it but as the path widened, women began to unite and have a voice. Once the pendulum began to move, it swung in extremes. Many women polarized to the masculine side, becoming much like the men they were attempting to free themselves from rather than expressing the beautiful balance of the masculine/

feminine energy. When energy has been out of balance for so long, the initial expressions are also out of balance. The experience of expressing freely needs time to find some level of equilibrium and realign with Source. The pendulum has swung back and forth many times, bringing us to a time of awakening to the true meaning of embracing the feminine, the goddess, the Divine Mother.

It is not only women who are beginning to free their souls. Men are coming to understand this essential aspect of their total being. It is the acceptance of our masculine and feminine aspects that will bring about the balanced life that exemplifies joy, abundance, and wellness. The light and love of our Spirit and the love and acceptance of our Will provides the Divine guidance that makes this so.

Free Will or False Will

The Will and its power are greatly misunderstood, equal to the misunderstanding of the feminine energy. The way of defining or attempting to understand the Will is often reduced to the unevolved ego, abuse of power, tyranny, or victimhood. These, and similar descriptions, are describing a false Will, the Will denied and judged, the feminine aspect denied and judged, responding to situations in life with desperation.

Whatever we are holding has a charge and maintains its form until it is released. An example of a charge held within, unaware, manifesting itself is seen in people attracting their worst fears. If the charge were released, a new perspective would light the way to end that pattern. The movement opens space, making it available for light, new information, new perspective, and understanding. As with all things held in denial, there is no light to see beyond the confines of judgment, pain, and falsehood. For the Will to be seen for what it is, it must be freed.

The Will must vibrate freely in order to survive and be what it is. The low compressed vibrations of a denied Will that is attempting liberation can be seen in the expression of violence, greed, judgments, survival, deceit, treachery, guilt, and fear in all corners of the globe. Any attempt of the Will to free itself releases the trapped emotions. To move what the Will has been forced to hold brings great criticism and judgment, yet it is exactly what must transpire for healing to occur. Conditioning in the Will must move or nothing new can be received.

When outside reality delivers a blow, many call it bad luck. What is happening is an attempt of the Will and Spirit to come together and find balance and acceptance. The charge that was held could no longer remain suppressed and, in a sense, it blows up. The emotions must be allowed movement, but I emphasize that personal responsibility for expressing these pent-up emotions must be taken for healthy change and evolution of the Will and the Spirit to be a sustainable reality. If our experiences are a vibratory match for skepticism and mistrust, then we have not embraced the understandings offered by the experience. Essentially, the experience is a missed opportunity for growth and will come around again at another time.

When I imagine the false Will expressing itself, I see an image of a wild animal that has been caged, pacing, hungry, and desperate to be free. The behavior is out of balance and disconnected from peace and Source. This representation is how some see the expressions of the Will, as wild, dangerous, and unpredictable. They cannot imagine the Will as a useful part of the self or of life. The Will is not only useful; it is essential. Our emotions are not only informative but also imperative to our wellbeing. This idea may not sit well with some folk; however, I do not believe I came to Earth to blindly conform. I do not think that was the design for any of us, and at this stage of our evolutionary process as a species, I can only hope we are digging deeper into everything that informs or educates.

Always remember, this process is about thought and feeling. We will have a difficult time if our growth is limited to an intellectual exercise, and we do not feel what lies within us as we explore expanded concepts of our own totality. Trusting ourselves leads to a lifetime of confidence, fluidity, humility, and grace. It leads to health, abundance, and happiness. I have been a seeker of truth since the age of three. It was in those pre-kindergarten years when I looked deep and long into my own eyes in a mirror and wondered who was in there. As I grew, I talked with God and wondered about God as I lay in the grass, watching the clouds form interesting shapes; as I listened to the birds sing and the water of the lake lap against the shore. I continue to commune with nature on a regular basis, to listen quietly to the sounds and feel the vibration of nature and her magic. Much can be learned, released, and understood in simple ways.

For those that find my experience and view of the Divine Mother, of our soul and the Will as one, to be some bit of nonsense or worse, I say we all must live our lives in ways that works for us. If you are having feelings about this, I just ask you to feel them and find out what they have to offer you. Emotions have a consciousness and when liberated, they provide valuable information for our growth. Set your soul free and listen. When we have grown enough to realize that experience is a great teacher, innocence and trust will be the guides. Each experience is unique unto itself when there is no judgment or denial blocking the way. If anyone feels emotions are inconvenient, rubbish, or of little to no importance, I give you thoughts from the writing of Sharon J. Wendt, PhD in her book *Healing the Heart, Healing the Soul*:

> Our emotions are the powerhouse of our human nature. They are the cornerstone of our creativity. Our emotions give us the ability to live our lives with passion. Out of this passion comes the creative genius in all areas of life: the arts, music, literature, invention, and science. Our emotions are there to guide us in our decision-making. Our emotions can be the compass for guiding our directions as we travel along the pathway of life. People, who are not in touch with their emotions, have no compass for their journey. They meander through life avoiding decisions or turning their decisions over to other people in their life. Or they make decisions based only on intellect, leaving out their heart.

For those of you who have found that many short cuts or quick fixes have not worked in a sustainable way, remain open and read on.

Conscious Mastery is about what I have experienced and what feels real to me. The more I liberate myself from dogma and the cruelty of judgment, guilt, denial, and false beliefs, the freer I have become to express myself honestly and make good choices. It is the small everyday choices that create a foundation for our ability to actively participate in our own health and wellbeing. The process of setting my Will free has made me aware of Divine Mother's important contribution to living a balanced life upon the Earth. It has brought me to a place of honoring Her through honoring my emotions and the information they bring. It has also brought me to honoring the Divine Father by honoring the light, inspiration, and action that assist in the process of creating a life that suits my soul. My Will, the magnetic energy associated with the feminine, has provided me with the ability to vibrate space open allowing light to expand my consciousness and raise the vibration of my thoughts and emotions, breaking patterns that were, in every sense of the word, killing me.

The innocence that is reborn brings the gift of light. Life can hold the wonder we knew and the delight we shared when we were children in simply *being*. Being childlike is not childish. Feeling self-love is not selfish. There is a different vibration that accompanies the latter. The more we clear ourselves of old charge, the easier it is to see and feel the difference. As Buddha told his disciples, "Be a light unto yourself." We will, one day, develop the capacity to make our way through the darkness, reclaim our right to be, and learn to live in harmony step by conscious step. As in the words of Mother Teresa, "The first step to becoming is to will it."

If we are disconnected from our feelings, we must begin to call our Will to us. A place must be made within us for our Will, the divine expression of our emotional nature. If we can accept our response to this, as well as accept the energy of the Will that moves to reconnect with us, we will find ourselves on the road to recovery. We will recover our right to be and to have. We will rediscover our gifts and our talents. We will recover our true deep connection with All That Is and our personal power. When our connection to Mother/Father God has been restored, balance is also recovered. We can feel it. Our Will, the Mother principle, desires to be in the light of God and feel the connection and acceptance in this alignment. When our Will is held in the darkness of denial, outside our own acceptance and God's love, it is a very painful place for our feminine principle to be. To feel and look honestly upon all of life's reflections provides important information that lights the way to realigning our self with Source.

My relationship with God is personal, as it is for many who come to desire a relationship with the Divine. Words from Lilly Tomlin come to mind; she said, "Why is that when people talk to God they call it prayer but when God talks to people they call it schizophrenia?" I laugh every time I read that but it is also sad. Yes, God does talk with us. If we have not heard Him yet and we desire to, we will. If we think it is impossible and believe his messengers, the Archangels or Wise Ones, communicate with us, then we can deepen our relationship with them. They will share the truth with us.

My personal relationship includes the Divine Mother, the magnetic, yin, emotionally intuitive creative aspect. It is the balancing of the masculine Father and the feminine Mother that brings heart essence into full bloom and expression. Our heart center is home to Divine Mother/Father God. The awakening of the Divine feminine, the Goddess, the Divine Mother by no means supersedes or excludes the Divine masculine, Father God. Balance is balance. Out of balance is out of balance. It does not matter if we are polarized to one side or the other; we are still out of balance.

When emotions are held rather than expressed, the Will is not free. The lack of freedom goes beyond the inability to express honestly and extends into the inability to receive new information and energy. The burden of holding, rather than expressing, honest feelings begins the manifestation of depression, as well as many other physical, mental, and emotional imbalances. When we free ourselves of this great burden we begin to experience honest feelings. As we begin to express ourselves honestly, it may feel a bit clumsy or even scary. Some of the expression will likely be out of balance; this is temporary. As we relax into expressing our own truth, balance will return. Expressing ourselves honestly and with kindness will become the way. The gift is natural Divine alignment of our Spirit and Will in harmony within the heart. Here love grows.

Balance Is Fluid

Balance is fluid. It does not adhere to a strict 50-50 contribution for all of life's experiences. Each and every situation and circumstance is unique. The best complementary blend of masculine and feminine energies is what will constitute balance. When we unconditionally accept all aspects of ourselves, we have both feet on the road to freedom. When both Spirit and Will are free, we can indeed experience balance in all areas of our life. We can see a harmony between inspiration, feelings, guidance, and action. The propensity to swing wildly from side-to-side ceases. This crazy-making comes to an end. Unity and peace within is felt in the balance that is played out in our ordinary, everyday, extraordinary lives. Unity and peace are reflected back to us, as our outer reality is a mirror, which reveals our inner landscape. As this comes to pass, we are consciously making use of our God-given internal guidance. Our Will is not separate from the Divine Will. We are not giving it up or giving it over. We are accepting it. Our Spirit is not separate from Divine Spiritual consciousness. We are opening space to receive it. The time to bring it all together is now.

"Balance is beautiful." Miyoko Ohno

Go To Bonus Media Center at:
http://www.ConsciousMastery.org/BonusMedia
To Download Bonus Media for Chapter Four

I Joyfully Let Go

CHAPTER FIVE

RELEASING, WHY AND HOW

What is releasing and why is it important?

To release judgment frees our minds; to release emotions frees our Will.

"Releasing" is the process of freeing trapped energy. Trapped energy goes by many names such as blockage, old charge, old baggage, repressed emotions, shadows, inner demons, and others. Releasing trapped energy begins the development of new perspectives and an expanded consciousness. Other benefits of releasing are renewed energy, patience, alignment with Source, personal power, greater health, lighter attitude, abundance and so much more. Emotion in its most natural state is energy in motion. Releasing pent-up emotions can be done consciously, yet it often occurs when we are triggered into a release by an experience. Conscious releasing begins with a desire for change. Recognition and acceptance of what has been denied set the transformation into motion. It is a path that brings an end to suffering and confusion closing the gap between Source and ourselves. It closes the gap between who we think we are and who we truly are. A successful release brings light to truthful feelings as well as a new way of seeing and living life in physical reality. Energy is consciousness. Vibrations hold information. Releasing consciously as a means of transforming energy brings about healing and a movement toward wholeness.

There comes a time when direct experience becomes the path and the answer. We can read and bring information into our minds, we can meditate and contemplate, all of which are valuable experiences unto themselves. Still, through it all, it is our ability to apply action to the knowledge we have gathered and to experience what we feel that makes this Earth walk so fascinating and rewarding. Our emotions must be allowed to move and evolve. When they do, they bring greater awareness and true understanding to the extent that we are open and ready to receive. The Will, as much as the Spirit, must evolve. In these times of heightened awareness, both the Will and the Spirit are attempting alignment with Mother/Father God. When we are aligned and reconnected with Source there is nothing about being in this world that does not reflect our Creator. Someone wise once said, "Show me where God isn't." The birth of compassion tells us He is everywhere. Releasing that which blocks the light from illuminating our consciousness and blocks us from the truth is the path I share throughout this book. Ideas and concepts of releasing are discussed in the chapters on denial, judgment, guilt, forgiveness, and others.

In this chapter are general ideas for us to use when we have decided to take the reins and the lead in our lives and to consciously move the energy that is ready to evolve. Having made such a decision will clear the way to live life with self-mastery. Transformation of energy can take place before something happens from our outer reality demanding change or shocking us as change sweeps us away. The energy of change is forever moving around and within us all. All we need do is decide to lead our life consciously into the flow of Divine Consciousness and put an end to the invisible forces that have been leading us into experiences that we are not ready for or do not desire.

Emotion, Energy in Motion

When emotions are moving, we do not have to make it "about" anything. Something or someone may have set them into motion, but once emotions are moving, let them move without dramatizing or amplifying drama. Surrender to the flow; breathe with and into the wave of moving energy. If the emotions that are moving inform you of something, acknowledge it. It is something useful or will be useful soon for your growth. Write it down. Flashes of insight are for those ready to receive them and ready to conceive a new way of seeing life unfold in all its beauty and simplicity.

Too often the opportunity to lighten gets lost in the mental framework of a story. If emotions are moving and nothing triggered their movement, we try to make them about something. Emotions begin to liberate themselves and move because they can, because somewhere along our path of making choices, we created an opening. We created an opportunity to embrace more understanding, more light, a greater desire to know more of who we are and be more of who we have always been. Allow the emotions to move unimpeded; too much thinking stifles the flow and blocks insight. Let go and see where they take you. Choose to be in a safe and comfortable place. Ride the wave, call in more light, you will not be disappointed.

Benefits of Releasing

Releasing the old charge of pent-up emotions can transform:
- Fear into faith. This allows fear to take its natural and right action of giving cause to examine an experience that we may or may not be ready for with faith enough to trust our intuitive feelings/guidance.
- Pain into passion, and the will to live life fully.
- Discouragement into perseverance.
- Weakness into strength and courage to change our lives for the better.

- Loneliness into healthy alone time. This opens space for a healthy relationship with ourselves, dissolving isolation as well as promoting healthy relationships with friends, coworkers, family, and new people.

Releasing old charge can reunite us with
- our personal power;
- our inner healer, promoting healing on all levels;
- our inner teacher;
- our inner child, promoting spontaneity, creativity, and honesty;
- our inner parent, informing us with emotional maturity and love.

Releasing old charge will
- lift us out of depression;
- broaden our consciousness;
- deepen our connection with Source, giving us the ability to feel and develop our fundamental nature, creating a way of life that resonates with joy, love, and peace;
- open the door for others to feel more comfortable about releasing and being honest with their own emotions, especially children;
- bring light to more of the truth;
- give us strength to grow and change our lives for the better;
- reignite the flame of passion and desire.

Signs that Energy Is Ready to Move

Not all releasing is painful, nor is it all about having outer reality trigger us with drama, trauma, or devastation. There are many creative and fun ways to move and evolve the energy we are releasing. Creative energy is extremely transformative. When approached with intent to move energy, creativity opens space for the inner child to express. This opens the door for amazing inner transformation.

Creative playtime for adults is a necessary part of a balanced life. This does not have to cost money. We can keep it simple; we can color, dance, roll on the floor, or cut up old clothes and make something new. Moving energy creatively must be carefree, without attachment to any idea of perfection. The intention is to move energy. Keep a journal handy, as thoughts will rise to offer insights on the journey of self-discovery. This will unlock the door to the treasure within.

As an example, you feel down, not at all like yourself. There is nothing going on in your life that seems to be the cause, in fact many things are really going very well. So why does this feeling tug at you for your attention? It could be that since everything is going well, you have created an opportunity for more goodness to find you. All you need is a little more room within and the old charge is asking you to let it move out. It could be sadness, fear or old judgments. Whatever it is, let it go and open a space for more light and more love.

Subtle energies that are ready to be released make themselves known in a variety of ways. We can feel uncomfortable in our bodies; our heads can feel thick, cloudy, or unclear. We can have uncommon body aches. There can be a general feeling of heaviness or heaviness in the heart. There can be a feeling of fatigue or slight depression. There can be anxiety or feeling of nausea. It can feel like intensity brewing, as the energy wants to expand. These are a few signs that tell us something is up. Something is reaching for the surface and is ready to move up and out and then to evolve into a higher vibration. Remember, energy is consciousness and vibration holds information. What has been contracted is attempting to expand. As the vibration increases, it offers new information. Give birth to a lighter, brighter you.

Embracing the concept that we are energy beings helps us become responsible for our energy. In this way, we can create a path that is lighter, joyful, intuitive, and more in line with our purpose, our destiny, and with Source.

A few other signs that let us know we are holding onto old charge and holding ourselves back from free Will: We consistently feel great resistance to going to work, are not happy there, and find ourselves getting sick often. We find little meaning in the things we do for the majority of our days. We feel bored. We are inclined to go to lengths to distract ourselves from feeling uneasiness, pain, anger, or unhappiness. We tolerate our relationships with our significant others or with most people, rather than enjoy them. We feel frequent anxiety. We frequently use sarcasm as a way of communicating. Our energy level is consistently low or bounces from one extreme to the other. We do not take good care of our general health. It is easy to find excuses to treat ourselves poorly, such as the denial of rest, proper food, and so forth. All of these are signs that energy is stuck or frozen in time, weighing us down, impeding our ability to think clearly and choose life-affirming action. It is time to lighten the load, thaw the emotional glacier, and learn to flow once again.

Some of the Basics

When we feel a need to move energy or energy is requiring our attention, and we intend to release consciously for the purpose of liberation, growth, and spiritual insight and to reconnect or strengthen our connection with Source, use the following list as a guideline to set the tone and the space.

- Always choose a place that is safe and comfortable.
- If you are doing this alone, choose a time and place you will not be disturbed or interrupted.
- If you are doing a release with someone facilitating, make sure there is a feeling of trust.
- If more than one person is releasing in a small group, be certain that everyone is on the same page and all feel safe with one another.
- Set the space. Make it personal for you. Choose your music, movie, creative supplies, or light a candle or incense. Use sage to clear the energy of the room. Use

a drum or clap your hands to break up any negative energy in corners of the room. All this brings you to the present moment, aligned with your purpose, and intent to connect and release.

- Have your journal, a pen, and drinking water ready.
- Wear comfortable, loose-fitting clothing, nothing tight or binding.
- While setting the space, keep your intention in the center of your heart and in the forefront of your mind.
- When the space is set, call in Mother/Father God or your guides and ask for protection, guidance, and assistance. These words of Paramahansa Yogananda come to mind, "A man of inspiration is humble…He knows he is a branch of the Divine Vine […] the branch cannot bear fruit of itself, except it abide in the vine." This reminds us that we are not alone. We are connected.
- Write your intention and then speak it out loud. "I intend to release XYZ. As the energy moves up and out, please purify and return to me as light."
- Always end with gratitude. Thank your guides. Thank yourself for taking the time. Be grateful. Smile. Walk with appreciation and the attitude of gratitude.

Integrate

If a good release has transpired, you may feel a bit tired. If so, rest and when you are ready, write in your journal. If you were able to write during the release, review what you have written. Do not sensor any thoughts or feelings that come up. It all has something to teach. Energy is consciousness and as such, our emotions have something to share with us. Acknowledge them but do not dwell in them. This is about releasing and letting go, so keep true to your intention. Add your new perspectives or desires to your journal writing. These insights are valuable. Take time to relax and appreciate what you have accomplished. With a sense of appreciation, write down what thoughts arose and what themes brought about the greatest release.

Many doors begin to open during this integration period. Be gentle and mindful. Listen to your inner voice. If the inner dialogue is less than soft and loving then gently raise it to match the vibration of self-love. Cradle yourself like a newborn babe. Trust in yourself and the process. Follow your internal guidance. It may take a few days for the entire download of awareness to find you receptive enough to get the full impact of the new understandings, so be patient. Remember that new understandings bring information that help shift perception. It may come as an awareness of something entirely new or it may clarify what you knew deep inside all along but were not ready to accept. Ideas for the next step may arrive in a flash of insight. Sometimes they come to us in dreams. Other times they dawn upon us slowly. These are a few reasons I emphasize journal writing and the importance of the process of integrating renewed energy. Energy is expanding; energy is consciousness. Your consciousness is expanding. Remain as conscious as possible to get the most of what this means for you. Everyone's journey is different and unique unto them.

There are times that the release can almost immediately make us feel as if a weight has been lifted. The process of integrating the new energy is just as important, whether we find ourselves quiet and introspective or bubbling up with new vitality. The latter can sometimes make taking the time to integrate a bit more challenging but it is nonetheless very important.

A word of caution, even if you feel like telling the whole world about your great experience, give it a little time to be with only you. Write this enthusiasm in your journal. It will be of great inspiration to you when you review it down the road. You are not being asked to repress your awesome high. You are only being asked to be responsible for the renewed energy that has returned to you. You are birthing more of your true self. Take care and nurture the energy, as you would a baby, to insure its strength and continued availability. In this way, the new energy will come home to rest in your heart center, sustainably raising your overall vibration to a higher level. After a time, the shift will be stable, and then, by all means, share what you feel inspired to share with whomever you feel inspired to share it with. Integration is covered in greater detail at the end of the chapter.

Well-Chosen Movies or Books

When struggling with old patterns of thought that drag us down or weaken the process of higher thinking, we can get into a book that is designed to inspire, inform, and bolster our inner strength. Reading books of this nature reminds us of what we innately know, lifts us quickly, and assists us in changing the direction of the downward spiral of negative thinking into the upward spiral of self-love. If we feel emotionally stuck or paralyzed, watching certain movies or diving into certain books can provide an opening for the energy to break through and to flow. Many of us who have intuitively done this know exactly what I am talking about.

A well-chosen movie could be just the medicine to get that old repressed energy to take flight. Ask in advance for more light to fill the space that is preparing to open and expand. Have some tissues, drinking water, and a journal handy. Then sit back and get into the movie.

A disconnection from true feelings happens when we have an experience that overwhelms the senses and the mind. In some cases, we withdraw from friends and family. Choosing a movie or book with the intention of breaking through can prevent a breakdown. When the emotions find their way to the surface, we then acknowledge the movement. Put down the book or pause the movie, allowing the energy to complete its movement. Call in light, drink some water, write in a journal and then resume the movie or book, if it feels appropriate. Healthy, conscious releasing can open the mind and free the emotions, bringing us back to life with a whole new perspective and renewed vitality.

Tears of Laughter, Tears of Joy

It is not only tears of sadness that can move with this method. We can also pick a funny movie to move energy with laughter. Some awesome, deep, belly laughs come with tears of unabashed joy and silliness running down our cheeks. Energy is in motion. Call in more light and be grateful. Not all release comes in waves that devastate us. In fact, if we are intending to broaden our consciousness, growing ever closer to the Divine, most release or clearing will be of our choosing, long before life bumps us on the head. The more old charge we clear, the more aware we are of subtle energy that is moving or ready to move.

As we free our emotional bodies, we also free our minds from the limited structures of old judgment and fear. Feelings and thoughts rising to a higher vibration is a path to setting ourselves free. Remember, this is a process of release not a distraction. Be mindful of what is stirring within and make this a worthwhile journey of great self-discovery, recovery of lost personal power, and reconnection with Source.

Music

Music is a powerful medicine. Music can lift our spirits and make our hearts sing. It also has the power to soothe the soul or fire us up. Music can bring about relaxation or aggression. As with all things, choose well.

To consciously intend to release using music as medicine, pick music that feels right. If we need some fire in the belly to get going, perhaps some tribal drumming or more high-spirited music will set us in motion. If we have access to hand drums and feel inspired to use them, by all means do. Drumming stirs much within us, bringing energy quickly into motion. The voice may take flight along with the sound of the drum. The body is involved and feels the power of the drum. Let go and flow with it. If we are listening to a recording, we can drum along using anything from a wooden spoon on a countertop to thumping on a pillow. If we are not inclined to drum along we can follow our breath as the music fills the room and our bodies. It is not unusual to feel the urge to move the body. Do not resist such urges; it is part of the process. Remember to always set an intention. An example could be, "I intend to drum, dance, sing, or breathe out the frustration of my workday or my confusion about my relationship or this feeling that I don't understand. May it be purified and return to me as light." Emotion is energy in motion. Allow it to express.

If we are already fired up and are close to being hotheaded, meaning likely to do or say things that would be regretted later, then we should choose something more soothing such as environmental sounds, easy listening, or even classical music. Music takes us to a place of releasing energy with Grace where we can feel our bodies slowly relax, be mindful of our thoughts, our breath, and our heartbeat. We can allow ourselves to unwind. This helps us to get grounded and come together. Too much fire can be dangerous; too little fire can be debilitating or depressing. As we become more aware of our thoughts, we must be sure to move them in the direction we want to go. If we have a thought of how much we dislike or hate something or someone, we cannot allow our thoughts to spin in this direction uncontrollably. We recognize the thought and then begin to raise it up. We might begin by saying or thinking, "I let you go, I forgive myself for holding on to this anger, and I choose to better understand this situation, light fill my heart, my thoughts, and my being."

In this way, we begin to rise up on the wave of the energy in motion and open to the understandings that are illuminating our consciousness. An example of a negative thought and its initial release: "I can't stand my job." Recognize the thought and the feelings surrounding this thought. You may be angry or sad and then an awareness of a higher thought such as, "I won't have this job forever." Do not push that thought away or ignore it. This is your first opening. Be with it and let it unfold. Continue to allow inspired thoughts to touch your awareness, taking you in a direction you want to go. In this case, it would be freedom from a job you do not like and the inspiration to create the necessary change. The opposite way to do this would be to dismiss the first uplifting thought with a plethora of reasons that keep you stuck such as, "I will never get another job, I have no choice, I can't quit, there is nothing out there." This is the path of spinning in the drama and amplifying the energy you are attempting to release. There is no progress in this. If you find yourself going in this direction, stop and course correct. Your thoughts may feel like wild horses going every which way but one simple thought can get you back the reins. You could think, "Wait a minute I do have choice. I will let my imagination unfold and show me other possibilities." Now you are back on track to releasing rather than spinning in the old pattern that no longer serves you or anyone else.

Body Movement and Dance

Allowing the body to move, with or without music, can be slow and easy like bending in the wind to wild and vigorous or anything in between. I have found that allowing the body to shake loose with feet firmly on the ground gives a sense of connecting with the body and the earth and brings attention to the present moment. The next step is letting the feet begin to move and to let the body move spontaneously. This is liberating, fun, and a good form of exercise.

Yoga is also a great way to allow energy that wants to move the freedom to do so and brings home the sense of unity and connectedness that is generally lost in fear and anxiety. Just about any form of exercise fits in this category, but I would like to emphasize making it something enjoyable with the freedom to be spontaneous as the energy begins to move. The free form dance is likely to be the most open and engaging but always tune in and find the best way for you. Again, set the intention. I like to have my pen and journal handy and will take a moment to write when something reveals itself. These revelations can come and go quickly.

Sound Using Voice

Let it be understood that when we grumble under our breath, let out sounds of exasperation, and make grumpy noise, unconsciously or consciously, it has nothing to do with releasing pent-up energy and is counterproductive. What we are doing is adding to the negative energy in our own field and all around us. It adds to the misery and negativity we are feeling. It reminds me of a vessel overloaded and out of balance, ready to tip over, affecting everything and everyone around it. We must be more conscious than this. When we speak, we should be conscious and speak kindly or remain quiet and realize the nature of our own thoughts. If our thoughts are of a low vibration, we can raise them up a notch or two or three. Bring our voice out in a way that is conscious enough to determine the course our energy will take. Sound a tone or sing a song that is healing, happy, child-like, and easy because it feels better; because we can; and because it is very healing. Even whistle a happy tune. Our voices are powerful tools to be used wisely.

With That Said

Using our voices creates a vibration in the body. The bigger the sound, the more easily it is felt but volume is not the focus here. You can begin with humming. It is getting our voice active and eventually out in the open that matters because it creates a vibration in the body. There are many chants and mantras available, which I highly recommend because they are aligned with high vibrations and have been sung for thousands of years with the intent of connecting to the Divine. There are techniques on toning that work beautifully when using the voice to assist with the releasing of energy.

When I use toning, I take the time to locate the energy that is tugging at me for my attention. Often I feel it in my belly, near the second and third chakras. Sometimes I feel it as a tightening in my throat chakra, perhaps letting me know something needs to be said. It can be anywhere. I have felt it as pain in the small of my back or in my shoulder, we cannot judge where we may sense the location, we just go with it. Wherever I find it is where I place my attention. I begin to make a small sound. It could be a hum, an ohm, an ah, or any sound that comes to mind. When the sound has begun, I imagine it touching that place within me that is ready to be released. I continue with the tone and let it grow according to the energy it is connecting with. Many times, the same tone is used until I need to draw another deep breath in and then begin again, slowly and determinedly, with my intention and attention. Always I am mindful of the energy moving in my body. If everything is speeding up, I let it. There are times when the voice wants to move in odd and interesting ways. This is creative energy expressing itself and I let it go where it wants. It is my voice and it loves to be free.

Releasing in this way is healthy, amazing, and empowering. When the release is complete, there is a gentle quieting or calm. Move into the calm and begin feeling your body, become aware of your thoughts. Toning can take on a life of its own. If the sound begins to shift and change, go where it leads you. An ah can transform into a song or sounds that are unfamiliar to you, a language of its own. Enjoy the freedom and let your voice out. It is one of my favorite ways to release energy. Do not bog yourself down with rules, judgment, or insecurities. Do not waste time limiting your freedom. Feel your personal power expand, increase its vibration, and align with Source. You can have all of these wonderful benefits through the release of your own voice.

Flow with Nature

We may choose to time our release session with the natural cycles of our Universe. All of nature and the cosmos have an ebb and flow. We may find it helpful to move in harmony with it. An example would be the cycles of the moon; full moon, new moon, solar eclipse, and lunar eclipse are powerful times and a great way to flow harmoniously with nature. In a general sense, the full moon is a time to let go of anything that no longer serves us, while the new moon is a perfect time to call in something new, such as opportunities, ideas, friends, and inspiration. We can create a simple ritual with a prayer, a candle, and our intention. By making ourselves conscious of the lunar cycles, we become more conscious of nature and the cosmos. It deepens our connection to the earth and the heavens. The changing of the seasons also brings powerful energy: the stillness and power of the equinox and the solstice. If we develop an interest in these cycles then it may be helpful to find an astrologer who offers information about the particular energies of each moon cycle, eclipse, and changing season. We can make the most of our conscious transformation of energy by riding on the natural tides provided by auspicious planetary alignments.

You could dedicate a piece of time to the new and full moon each month. This would develop your personal connection to the rhythm of nature and the heavens. You can begin with something as simple as lighting a candle and quieting your mind. There is a wonderful feeling of connectedness that occurs when we pause from the daily hustle and bustle to relax with the moon. You do not have to have something pressing to release to grow from this experience. A few examples for the full moon could be, "I am willing to release anything I am holding that no longer serves my highest good. I am willing to release and transform all energy that is ready to go. I am ready to release any inappropriate relationships or activities that no longer serve my highest good." A few examples for the new moon might be, "I am open and willing to receive a new opportunity for my growth. I am open to receive more love. I am open to receive, feel, and sense new inspirations when they come to me with greater awareness."

Keep in mind energy is always flowing. When you release with the full moon take the time to breathe in light and love. When you are bringing in energy with the new moon, take a moment to breathe out any energy that may be standing in the way.

Keep It Simple

Make the decision to get outside and commune with nature. It is magical, powerful, and transformative. As with all release, set an intention then get outside, breathe the fresh air, and connect. It is a wonderful way to release pent-up energy, to find the reservoir of peace within. Listen to the sounds, take in the sights, walk, run, bike, or sit under a tree in your backyard and meditate. There is an unspoken magic in nature that helps draw out our lower vibrations. Nature can assist us with releasing pent-up emotions. Consciously intend to shift your energy to a higher vibration, feel the movement, and enjoy the nature that surrounds you.

Involvement in Something Creative

There is no end to the ways in which we can express ourselves creatively, but many people have forgotten just how simple it can be. When was the last time we drew a picture for the fun of it or colored with crayons? When we want to use creative expression as a way to release and evolve our energy, we set and keep our intention in our heart center as we prepare our space with whatever supplies we need. Remember, this is about releasing and shifting energy from a lower vibration to a higher one. There is no room to judge our creations. If we find ourselves doing that here is our opportunity to release those debilitating thought forms. We must treat ourselves with the same kindness we would treat a child trying something for the first time. Let that old, inner critic go, release it, and have fun.

Attuning to the End of a Release
Ebb and Flow

With all things there is an ebb and flow; releasing consciously is no exception. There may be times when we may feel resistance to completing the process. We must acknowledge it and reaffirm our intention and purpose out loud, breathe consciously, and continue. The mind may try to convince us to abandon the process tempting us with "I should this" and "I can't that" but we must not fail prey to the old pattern. And to the best of our abilities, we continue to persevere until we are really done. I remember days when thoughts of cleaning the toilet would take me away from creative passions and conscious releasing. While I was there cleaning I would think to myself, "what in the world is wrong with my priorities?!" The answers came as they always do.

Heightened Awareness

Attuning to the end of the release is easier to do when the release is done consciously, as opposed to being triggered by outer reality. Nonetheless, it is important to feel the subtle shift of the release coming to an end. What you will notice is a calm or quiet coming over you. Move with the calm and be quiet. Rest and wait. Notice how your body feels, notice the slow thoughts that rise up into your awareness. These are worth writing down in your journal. Do not censor your thoughts. You may not understand them at the moment but as your consciousness expands, clarity will come. Sometimes it is like new puzzle pieces finding their places. When the energy begins to calm, move with the calm, do not attach to drama and amp up the energy unnecessarily. It would be wise to ask yourself, "Is this release complete at this time?" If round two rises up naturally then go with it.

Note: Forcing or pushing the energy up to another level is more likely to happen when you are triggered into releasing by another person and you remain in the presence of this person while releasing the pent-up energy. This is not recommended. It is better to walk away from the trigger and return when you have regained your balance. If you are truly releasing, truly setting your Will free with intent to grow, evolve and align with Source, no harm will come to anyone and that includes you.

Anything New

If we are releasing and releasing and still not receiving greater understandings or new perspectives, a few possibilities exist. One is that there is something underneath what we are releasing that we have yet to acknowledge. For example, we continue to release anger and seemingly get nowhere. Perhaps what is still being denied is the fear underneath the anger. Releasing anger over and over with no results is akin to dealing with a symptom rather than the cause. In this case, the cause is fear while the symptom is anger.

Another possibility is that we are acting out the energy and amplifying it rather than releasing it. We will know by paying attention to the stillness that follows or if there is a stillness. If all we have coming to us are regrets, more anger, and sorrow, we might discover we have amplified the energy and cleared nothing. This is not altogether a waste of time, if we can see this result. Regardless of how we moved our energy, we need to learn something from it. If all we learned is the need to find a safe place to express then we have learned a great deal. If we have discovered some release cannot be done in the face of the person that triggered it, we have learned a great deal. Do not blame or shame but rather contemplate what would be a better way to move the energy next time.

Take to heart these understandings. Write them in a journal. You will be surprised at the inspired thoughts that will find you if you intend to grow and remain open. Be kind to yourself and love yourself. This will set you up to handle your release in a more conscious manner, with your own best interest at heart, which in turn is the best for everyone. You can always ask for more assistance from Source, your angels, guides, or a trusted friend or facilitator. Remember as the energy begins to move, it is your responsibility to be open for the information your Soul longs to share with you. Energy is consciousness and vibrations hold information. Stay open for new perspectives. Direct your thoughts toward the light and love.

Devoting your time to a formal release will shed light on new ways of thinking about and living your life. You will reclaim more of your personal power. The next step will present itself. It always does. It may show up in the form of an opportunity, insight, new person, or heightened awareness. Lighten up, it feels good.

Integration

Integration is such an important part of the releasing process that I brought the idea to your attention in the beginning of the chapter. Integrating renewed energy is honoring the restoration of lost Will as we grow to experience a greater sense of wholeness. It may feel as if we finally brought home to our hearts lost or forgotten parts of ourselves. We must treat ourselves lovingly. This is so important. Letting go of old harmful patterns makes room for more of who we truly are. It restores parts of us that may have fragmented or were lost in the darkness of denial. If we are going to spend our time and energy letting go of old charge, denial, judgments, and destructive patterns of behavior, it stands to reason that we would want to do what is necessary to stabilize the renewed energy. Keep in mind the energy that returns to us is ours and always has been. Any energy we release that does not return was not ours. It is interesting to note as a singular example that through the process of adhering to someone else's beliefs, we can actually be holding energy that is not even ours. Releasing opens the opportunity for all energy to find its right place. Our energy returns to us as usable, loving, productive energy.

When you have completed a release, whether it is formally as in setting the space consciously, or was brought about by a trigger from outer reality, caring for yourself enough to honor the temporary feeling of emptiness that occurs after a release is a must. Do not try to fill yourself up with distractions. All you need do is wait with love and patience. You will recognize the return of your renewed higher vibration. This waiting period is essential to stabilizing and sustaining your re-qualified energy.

It is important to listen to and honor the needs of the body. If you are tired, rest. If you feel energized, consciously choose an activity that is creative, lighthearted, and fun. Let the energy move in playful ways that are light in both their content and execution. You may feel inspired to do something that you have only allowed yourself to think about before. Let your inner child come out and play. This is not a time to be reckless; it is a time to nurture. It is not a time to demand perfection; it is a time to play with complete abandon.

Whether you are full of energy or needing rest, providing the body with plenty of water is far more important than most think. Your body is made up largely of water. Releasing and moving energy is often accompanied by increased heat, the fire element, and the release of toxins. Often there is shedding of tears or sweat, the water element, both of which can dehydrate the body. Hydrate your body with water and help it move the toxins out so your physical body may easily come into balance. Preparing and feeding the body light healthy food with the attitude of gratitude assists the process of integrating higher vibrational energy. It is a natural way of sending messages of love to your body. This is a good time to take up the practice or continue with the practice of blessing your food and feeling grateful before eating. Eat mindfully, with appreciation for what you have before you.

Before getting into the rest of your day, give yourself the gift of time. Approach whatever tasks you have at hand, regardless of how important or mundane they may seem, with the softness that accompanies our energy bodies after a release. No pushing or demanding, just flowing and going with the flow. Notice what feels different.

The integration portion of releasing involves the mind. It has stretched beyond the normal confines of the old pattern. Take the time to write your thoughts and your experiences in your journal. This is most effective when done daily or spontaneously through out the day as new thoughts and insights illuminate a mind that has just expanded. It is wise and prudent to care for this growing ground by carefully discerning forms of entertainment. I highly recommend taking time off from watching the news, television, as well as movies with violence and dark content. Quiet time is preferred; time to reflect, to write, and to feel. Feed the mind with uplifting thoughts either of your own making or by choosing some good reading. The mind is an amazing tool when you take the reins and lead the power of the mind in the direction of your choosing. Dance to the tune of personal growth, increased happiness, self-discovery, new awareness of hidden talents, joy, vitality, health, self-reliance, and a sense of unity, and the beat goes on.

Conversations involving gossip, hate, and depressing topics should be placed outside the boundary of your new growing ground. It is amazing how many people fulfill a need within them by sharing horrifying information or vicious gossip. Take the lead in your life and walk away from such energy-draining talk. It is all right to let the other person or persons know you are not interested in that particular topic. It gives them the understanding that individuals can choose and are not subject to ongoing chatter that silently steals away time and energy. Care for your energy, your space, and your time. You have the power of choice.

Patience is a wonderful by-product in the process of evolving. There are many changes that take place as our consciousness expands. It takes time to see those reflected back to us. Stay true to yourself. If you ever feel like the old way is nipping at your heels take a moment and review your journal, bolster your inner courage, remind yourself of how far you have come and what has changed. Remember to care for all aspects of expanding awareness and illuminating consciousness like you would a newborn, then a toddler, and so on. Growth can be quick. You must honor the work you have done and remain open to continue when the time is right. Ask yourself if you are ready for another session of releasing. This is a journey with no end. That excites me because life would lose some luster, mystery, and magic if I thought I knew all there was to know. Embrace the mystery and enjoy the journey. It is ongoing!

Wrapping It Up

The more we release old patterns that have the outside world dictating to us, the easier it becomes to know our own thoughts and to stand up for ourselves. The rebirth of personal power is something to be aware of, care for, and bring home to the heart. This requires us to be interested and accountable for our lives as well as to embrace new awareness with the innocence and wonder of a child. No one would willingly expose a child to a harsh environment. We would be wise to embrace our new growing ground with the same care. Nurture the self. The more love we bring home to the heart, the stronger and more flexible we become, and the sooner we are ready for the next level of freedom from the bondage of old patterns, old limitations, and old judgments. Soon we begin to realize how fluid energy is and how much power we have to choose the life we live. It becomes clear that we grow in waves or stages and the time to integrate the new wave of energy is just as important as the release.

"Three things cannot long be hidden the sun, the moon, and the truth." Confucius

Go To Bonus Media Center at:
http://www.ConsciousMastery.org/BonusMedia
To Download Bonus Media for Chapter Five

I Plant the Seed of Forgiveness

CHAPTER SIX

FORGIVENESS

"An eye for an eye makes the whole world blind." Gandhi

Forgiveness is a key to freedom and liberation of the soul and the spirit. Forgiveness is the starting point where wounded heart essence can begin, once again, to vibrate at the rate of love. Increased vibration of heart essence expands and opens the heart. Heart essence is unconditional love and unconditional acceptance. Heart essence is the balance of our masculine feminine aspects. It is the dwelling place of Mother Goddess/Father God. This is where the expression of love from Source springs forth in all directions and in all ways always. Here in the heart, light, love, and acceptance, expand expressing love through us in a balanced and harmonious way. We begin to feel the flow of life rather than the struggle of life. When circumstances change, we begin to see the opportunity rather than the obstacle. This beautiful dance of ever expanding love and consciousness is the gift held within the seed of forgiveness.

Planting the seed of forgiveness in the dark areas of our hearts precedes the gestation and birth of a healed, healthy, open heart vibrating at the speed of light and love. And like the birth of anything, the birthing of heart essence requires nurturing into maturity. When we express freely, honestly, and truthfully from a place of great heart essence, it is a reflection of emotional maturity and balance. It is kind, gentle, and powerful. Attempts to grow beyond our self-created limitations will fall short if forgiveness is ignored, shunned, or not introduced into the process of healing and transformation.

We must plant a seed of forgiveness in the dark, formidable, forgotten gap between ourselves and our true Source. This gap is the place we will find our denial, our judgments, our hatred, and our buried fears and guilt. Its unseen weight is heavy upon the soul, the body, and the spirit. If we were to look deeper within or were willing to look objectively at what life is reflecting, we would have eyes to see the unseen and ears to hear words unspoken.

Forgiveness Begins with the Self

As with every step taken into the light of the new day, forgiveness begins with the self. Always beginning with the self is not a selfish process; it is a process of healthy self-love and taking responsibility for our lives. Without forgiveness we can become bitter, vengeful, hard, depressed, and lose hope of ever finding the wellspring of joy that resides within us. Hope is one of the great and powerful tributaries of love. Forgiveness is another. Unconditional acceptance is another. If any one of these tributaries is blocked, it has a detrimental effect on all others. The flow of love becomes stifled and sometimes blocked altogether. It does not mean love is not there. It means we are not letting love in. Without love there is heartlessness. It is in the pit of heartlessness that the seed of forgiveness must be introduced. It is not enough to have vibrating heart essence for only certain areas of our lives or for only certain people or some of our experiences. Heart essence must vibrate for all of life. Where heart essence is not vibrating, heartlessness draws more dark experiences into itself. The greater the gap between self and Source, the more challenging, sorrowful, depressing, guilt-ridden, lacking, confusing, and hateful our life expression become. The path of swinging from heart essence to heartlessness is difficult to walk and makes creating our heart's desire unpredictable at best.

Withholding Love

Withholding love is the transition or swing from heart essence to heartlessness. When things become challenging and nothing seems to be going your way, do you withhold your love? If someone is not doing what you hope for, expect, or demand, do you withhold your love? You may ask, "What does that mean or what does that look like?" It looks like many things. It can be taking something back or giving something back to someone with intent to cause pain; refusing to give a hug; saying or thinking mean things with intent to hurt another; falling short of your own expectations and hurting your body with excessive eating, alcohol, or drugs; denying your body food to punish yourself or someone through your suffering. Also, the use of the silent treatment is a cruel withholding of love.

These examples may seem minor but expressing heartlessness, withholding, or withdrawing love is never minor. It is cause for great suffering. We do it to others and we do it to ourselves. It is time to stop this unconscious practice of expressing heartlessness, see it for what it is and to consciously practice the art of expressing love by expanding heart essence. To share love when everything is well in our world is wonderful. To share love when it is not is Divine and an expression of compassion and emotional maturity. Even anger can be expressed from a loving heart. It is love that tempers the anger to assist in appropriate expression with openness to understand and seek balance.

More obvious examples of heartlessness are violence, vengeance, verbal abuse, and emotional abuse. Whether we inflict pain upon ourselves or someone else, we are coming from a place of heartlessness. Revenge never satisfies and never evens the score. Fairness is never found, as the vengeful are blind to it. Revenge and other heartless behaviors bind the perpetrator to the victim.

Intend to Forgive

Forgiveness begins with the intention to forgive the self and sets us free from the bondage, hooks, and weight of the past. To look to the past, through the eyes of forgiveness, for what can be learned, understood, and reclaimed, allows the present to become more open for change, freedom, love, creativity, and prosperity. The inception of forgiveness brings stifled heart essence into a vibratory state that will come to match the light and love from whence it came. Once the intention has been set and agreed upon within ourselves and the seed has been planted, the process of vibrating love into the darkness begins. Much of what will vibrate here does not feel good initially. It is our trapped, forgotten, and denied Will, our very soul feeling this opportunity to move and regain power through the inception of forgiveness. The crippling of the Will destroys the natural ability to relate, convey, and share the truth. Reclaim what has been denied. The Will desires to embrace life in the light of love and dies a slow death in the darkness of denial vibrating ever more slowly as time passes. We were not designed to wither and die as powerless victims of circumstances or cruel tyrants viewing all opportunity for growth as life's misfortunes.

Emotional Conditioning

Unfortunately, we have been conditioned to do what ever it takes to only feel good. Of course this is an illusion, yet this is why many of our emotions are denied and why many people do not follow through with clearing old charge. We are deeply caught up in the good/bad labels of emotions, having strong preference for good ones. Allowing feelings to move freely is not something that many humans practice. Keep in mind when we are living a life of limitation, limiting our emotional expression, what we believe feels good is extremely limited. The choices made to deny, judge, and fear much of our lives and ourselves makes this so. The journey to wholeness is bringing all our parts together into the light of love. When lost or fragmented parts of ourselves return home to our hearts, we may feel out of sync with our physical body. This can take the form of flu-like symptoms, increased agitation, headaches and the like. The vibration is a bit off but is rising up to regain resonance and balance with love. We must nurture and care for these lost parts until they are transformed, healthy and integrated into the whole of us. To do this, we need to take care of our bodies with rest, light food, plenty of water, get fresh air, meditation, and fresh juice. Keep in mind we are recovering. We are recovering lost parts of ourselves, lost energy, and talents. We are recovering our lost or broken connection with Source. We are recovering from the disease of illusions, separation, and denials.

Forgiveness begins to grow within the heart, bringing about the process of birthing more heart essence. Acceptance can be regained in the light of forgiveness. We must nurture our feminine aspect and our heart as we would our own child. Our inner child needs tenderness and patience. As love grows, heart essence expands becoming capable of expressing a complementary balance between divine thought and true feelings. This expansion of the heart allows Mother/Father God to express through us more fully. Action and receptivity blend and balance in appropriate behavior. Transformation or healing, one and the same, will raise our vibration to a higher frequency. We begin to experience the beauty and natural flow of right place-right time. What we thought felt good before will pale next to the experiences we will have when our heart expands, vibrating more heart essence. Heartlessness is transformed, becoming the love that longs to flow through us.

Why Should I or How Can I?

Are you asking why you need to forgive yourself? Are you feeling like the victim in your life's story? Are you asking, "How could I be forgiven for what I have done?" Are you feeling guilt or shame? The scenarios in life where forgiveness would liberate an individual are as many as there are individuals. No matter what has occurred in your life, the only place you can truly start the process of forgiveness and ultimately your own transformation, is with the self. Forgive yourself for holding onto the painful past and resisting the lesson. Forgive yourself for holding the weight of resentment from a past experience. Forgive yourself for holding the weight of shame or blame of yourself or someone else for what has happened. Forgive yourself for holding anger, rage, or hatred for someone or something from the past. Forgive yourself for holding fear of the past. Forgive yourself for holding guilt and allowing guilt to run your life. Forgive yourself for denying yourself joy, love, adventure, and pleasure because you hold a false belief of your unworthiness. Perhaps you are holding secrets that haunt you or holding secrets for others that are too heavy to bear. Forgive yourself for allowing the past to weigh heavily upon your mind, body, soul, and spirit, depriving you of precious energy that could be channeled into joy and purpose. Forgive yourself for holding the past that affects your today and your tomorrows. Forgive and live. You have nothing but heaviness to lose and everything that is light to gain.

Forgiveness and Acceptance

The energy that will transform with forgiveness is the energy held in a state of denial. Many of us do not know or even remember what we are holding but this does not stop the energy from playing out in our lives. It is outside our current state of consciousness. Another gift forgiveness brings is awareness of what we have been holding. Forgiveness is the starting point where heart essence can begin to vibrate at the rate of light and love. This higher vibration expands the heart. Vibration brings information. The light brings recognition by illuminating consciousness. Recognition and acceptance precede transformation.

At some point in our lives the old outworn patterns break or we break. If the pattern breaks as a result of our conscious work to forgive, to clear, and to transform our energy then it is a breakthrough. Consciously releasing trapped energy paves a way for us to embrace forgiveness in ways that once seemed impossible. The impossible becomes possible, as the essence of our Will is free to express itself. Breaking through the patterns is the path of liberating our souls. If we break after much continued holding of the past, it is typically a breakdown. The latter is the reflection of resisting the lessons and clearly the more difficult path home to the heart. Sooner or later, the seed of forgiveness must be planted if we are to reclaim what has been lost. Much of what has been lost to us is our connection to Source, personal power, hopes, dreams, health, and guidance. We need to let ourselves off the hook and swim free in the ocean of love.

As forgiveness takes root, life feels as though a weight has been lifted because it has. Forgiveness feels like fresh air and a renewed sense of freedom. Forgiveness disentangles our energy from the cause of turmoil, suffering, and lack. Acceptance holds out a hand to lift us up, not because we agree with what happened but because we can accept that it did. Acceptance precedes the release of all that ails us. We accept the behavior and forgive ourselves for resisting the lesson. This is not to say we continue to allow or deliver harmful behavior. It is to say that we accept the behavior that has occurred and through acceptance, learn the lesson and stop the painful pattern of behavior from expressing in our lives. It is when we let go that we regain and recover all that has been lost to us. Entanglements deplete our vital life force, our energy, and our personal power. The cause of turmoil may be insidious and unclear but that does not diminish the weight it accumulates as we do not or cannot accept that it exists. Entanglements of this nature are like a stranglehold on our creative life force. Entanglements cloud our minds from the truth and blur our good senses. The effects are eventually carried over into every area of life and this includes the health of our physical bodies.

To attempt to even the score and make things right from our perspectives further deepens and strengthens the entanglement. Similarly, if we struggle to acceptance rather than choose to accept, the struggle strengthens the bonds that restrict movement both figuratively and actually. Movement, rather than restriction, is what sets us free. If we are adamant about not forgiving ourselves, something, or someone we have our starting point. We begin with releasing the belief that we are somehow justified in our choice to not forgive. It does not serve us, our highest good, or anyone else. We soften the stubborn judgment and free our emotions of fear, anger, or whatever emotion holds this belief in place and then set ourselves free. When we cannot or will not forgive, we suffer. We have suffered long enough.

The more honest we become with ourselves, the more accepting we become of our experiences and ourselves. Everything has something to teach us. The liberation of our Will opens space for understanding. This lights the way to allowing forgiveness to do what it does so well, which is to free us from our self-created bondage. If we start with the intention to plant the seed of forgiveness, more of the original cause of confusion, chaos, and suffering will be made known to us. This is good because now we can let it go. We can feel what needs to be felt and nurture the seed of forgiveness with what love we have. Love will surely grow and with more love the capacity to forgive grows. Release immediately all thought of blaming, shaming, judging, self-hate, and guilt. Let go and ask Mother/Father God for help transforming this energy into the light of love. What belongs to us will return to us as love and light. When we have successfully forgiven ourselves for holding the pain and shame for what we have done or what has happened to us, we discover the ability, the love, and the inner strength and wisdom to truly forgive. If forgiveness of the self is insincere or incomplete, forgiveness of others is equally insincere. It is not by words alone that forgiveness resonates true. Begin with the self and all else will naturally unfold in time.

Plant the Seed

To have gone through this process at least once opens the door to understanding the importance of forgiveness and paves the way to continue. It becomes clear how we are hurting ourselves by holding pain, grudges, vengeance, guilt, and more. It becomes clear how we are the recipients of great light, love, joy, and a sense of renewal as our hearts expand naturally in the process of forgiveness. We gain insight to put an end to old patterns. It becomes easier to accept what has happened and let it go. We discover that to forgive what has happened allows the experiences of the past to become the wellspring of wisdom that they were always meant to be, instead of a stagnant, debilitating pool of denial, pain, and regret. As we grow, we align with the Divine and our choices reflect this loving alignment. Our God-given internal guidance system guides us to the right place at the right time and inspires us into right action. The flow has truly begun. Forgiveness has unlocked the door to the freedom and liberation of our souls. It has set into motion the expansion of our hearts. Open the door of your heart. Plant the seed of forgiveness. Nurture the seed with tender, loving care.

"The alchemy of forgiveness soothes the soul."
Lyric from a song I wrote many years ago called "Philosopher's Stone"

Go To Bonus Media Center at:
http://www.ConsciousMastery.org/BonusMedia
To Download Bonus Media for Chapter Six

I Accept Myself Just As I Am

CHAPTER SEVEN

Denial Is Not Our Friend

We can neither control nor transcend what we deny.

Self-Acceptance, A Key to Our Wholeness

Self-acceptance is the ability to lovingly receive and be all that we are with grace. All that we are, is the sum total of all the gifts given to us by our Creator, Mother/Father God. It is the expression of our physical selves, the light of our spirits, the love of our souls, the sweetness of our hearts expressing on Earth as the individuals we know as ourselves.

As sound as it may seem or as easy as it may sound, living and loving ourselves with complete acceptance is rare. The moment we begin finding fault with our bodies, holding back our true feelings, disguising our true natures, we have lost the alignment of self-acceptance. With this lost alignment, we grow to become something we are not. A string of events occur that will continue to take us further from our destiny and our true selves unless the events are seen for the opportunities for growth that they really are. Most people see it as bad luck when it is an opportunity to regain our lost alignment.

Integrity is the state of being whole and undivided. Where there is a lack of acceptance for the self, there is a lack of the integrity within the true self. We cannot be whole when we love, care for, or nurture only parts of ourselves. A lack of acceptance creates a weakening in the energy field. The three heavy weights, denial, judgment, and guilt, along with a big dose of fear will penetrate the weak spots and begin the process of weighing heavy upon the body, mind, spirit, and soul. This begins to fragment the true self. The God-given internal guidance system becomes dysfunctional along with our emotional expression. Our life experiences become heavy, making us feel every bit the slave or prisoner to the demands of the invisible forces of denial, judgment, and guilt.

Similar to any addiction, this usually happens in small increments. Little by little, relatively unnoticed, we lose more of our true selves as we find fault with who we are. The thought of not being enough begins to scrape away at the integrity of our very wholeness. We create or adopt a persona that we believe to be better than our true selves and may make us feel safe. We choose to believe in the illusion, hoping to find acceptance from the world. This cannot happen when self-acceptance is lacking. A vibrational match for a lack of acceptance is what will present itself sooner or later.

There is often a quiet hope that being something other than who we are will get us something. Anything achieved in this way cannot last because the foundation is based on a false representation of the self. Beyond the veil of forgetfulness, we grow unaware of the fact that we are not who we really are. However, in these fast-paced, changing times, the true self begins to stretch, nudge, and grow impatient. Many people are feeling it and hearing the call. Questions arise that inspire many people to look for answers. Questions like: "Who am I really? What am I doing with my life? Why am I so unhappy?" Look within. The answers are waiting for us there. Statements such as, "I know I am so much more. I can do better than this" begin to surface. As uncomfortable as it may be, it is a good sign. It is the awakening. Are you feeling the wake up call to remember who you are?

Do not fade away, becoming more of something you are not. Begin the art of loving yourself just as you are today and let that love grow. You will discover you have always been enough; you are wonderful and beautifully unique. You are a divine child of a most loving creator. You are experiencing spiritual awakening, spiritual awareness, and transformation on every level.

I speak of acceptance frequently throughout this book because self-acceptance is key to positive change and growth. Your life expression thus far may find you not liking what you see in yourself. That is really quite all right. Just do not let it stop you from accepting it. You can accept what is without liking it. Remember: acceptance of the self as you are right now is the key to positive change. Allow self-acceptance to become your ally and assist you on your journey home to the heart of all you are. With that said let's look at what is not your friend.

Denial Is Not Our Friend

Denial gains a foothold through our inability to accept our experiences and ourselves. The denied aspects of the self are hidden from our current state of consciousness. These denied parts of the self are in the dark and constitute much of what is commonly called shadows or inner demons. All aspects of the self that are hidden in the dark are outside the light of God's love, which provides nourishment in the form of understanding, awareness, hope, joy, peace, and inner strength. The lack of light causes us to be blind and unaware of what messages we are vibrating out into the world and disconnect us from the understandings that could free us from unhealthy patterns. Where there is emotional blockage, there is denial and old judgments widening the gap between Source and ourselves. The gap sets us apart from our authentic selves and from each other, losing the sense of unity and oneness.

When we tell ourselves something is not happening when it is, or something is happening when it is not, we do not have acceptance for what **is** happening. When we cannot accept what is happening, we were not ready for the experience in whole or in part and are overwhelmed.

The experience is denied and sometimes forgotten. Judgments are then created to provide a false sense of control and knowledge.

A Simple Example

A person, Mary, gets fired from her job for having a poor work ethic. The inability to take responsibility for her conduct in the work place may have her making excuses. The judgment could be something like, "I was fired because they are envious of me." Here we see someone who is not accepting the experience for what it is and creating a judgment that allows her to feel a false sense of righteousness and control. The wall created by the judgment will hold or suppress the true emotions of fear and shame giving strength to the judgment. This, in turn, gives strength to the denial rather than the truth, which is that the job loss was a result of a poor work ethic and had nothing to do with envy. In a state of denial, the situation is not seen for what it is and nothing is being understood or learned. Thus denial opens the door for judgments, misunderstandings, emotional blockage and all such limitations and conditions that keep us separate from the truth. Denial is further strengthened and held in place by self-imposed emotional control, in Mary's case in the example, suppressing and controlling the emotions of fear and shame as well as the very judgments that were created to justify the denial. Similar situation will follow until the experiences are seen for what they and the lesson is learned. In this case, the lesson would be that moral conduct in the work place is essential to continued employment.

Once a denial is recognized, the fastest way to end it is to release the judgment and free the trapped emotional energy. The recognition is that Mary's getting fired had nothing to do with envy and everything to do with a lack of moral conduct on the job. She can put an end to denying responsibility for the lost job, release the judgment, feel and then free the repressed energy of fear and shame that can now move and evolve into a higher vibration. Feeling what needs to be felt will bring light to the situation opening the gateway for understanding, which provides a way for Mary to make choices in the new job that are ethical. With denial seen for what it is and the judgment and emotions released, the liberated energy can move freely and add to her personal power instead of diminishing it. Once a lesson has truly been learned and understood it no longer repeats itself.

When and How Denial Begins

Denial always begins with lack of acceptance. It begins as soon as we are old enough to believe we are not good enough or are having experiences that overwhelm us. When we are born we are in the hands of earthly caregivers, too often our Will is broken when we are very young. The Will, associated with our feelings and personal power, is a necessary aspect of the total being. The loss of personal power and innocence are accompanied by a loss of our ability to sense our inner world. Our internal guidance is interrupted and as children we do know that we need those outside of us (i.e. caregivers) if we are to survive. This does not necessarily come about by cruel parents. Often, the caregivers were doing their best but were unaware of the unconscious patterns motivating them.

Today adults young and old are still operating by unconscious patterns, unaware of what is motivating them to do as they do. The difference now is the amount of resources and information available for those who truly seek to understand what drives them and why. If we are attracting experiences or people we do not want and would prefer to create what we do want, we start with believing in ourselves. Believe that we know what is not working in our lives. Believe we have what it takes to change the things that are not working. Believe we will discover our authentic selves. Believe that we know what is best for us and what we desire, even if it is buried in the subconscious and out of reach in the present state of consciousness. Believe we can feel what needs to be felt and we will not only survive, we will begin to thrive. Our personal power and our ability to create the life we desire will not remain buried and out of the light of our awareness if we have intent to know ourselves, to evolve, heal, transform, and be fully empowered.

In my quest for truth, I eventually grew to remember what seems to be my first entanglement with denial. Of course, I did not know what it was then; I was very young. I was experiencing great fear and emotional pain at home, a place I should have felt safe. I was an extremely sensitive child and felt things very deeply, much to the annoyance of nearly everyone around me. One day it occurred to me that if I threw that feeling, that thought, that memory into the back of my mind, it did not hurt anymore. Wow, what a great discovery. Or was it?

Denial occurs when life presents in ways that are too overwhelming to accept. It happens in our innocence, and we are unaware of the damage that is caused and will continue to be caused as denial opens the gateway for judgments, misunderstandings, emotional blockage, illusions, manipulation, and all other conditions and limitations placed upon our energy and the truth. The denial begins to break down the connection we have with Source. Even if, as children, we were not entirely conscious of or knew what this beautiful connection was, it was present, strong, and true. Sadly, it does not take long to become lost in our physical reality, with its twisted sense of truth, rules, doctrines, and fear-based thinking.

For me, denial was an act of survival that I embraced as a child because it appeared to bring some relief. As a child, I felt no safe place for expressing my love, my anger, fear, growing resentment, and even hate for all the discord present in my home. I had thoughts of how bad I was to have these feelings and punished myself with an ongoing, personally debilitating, inner dialogue. I had no skills or confidence to give myself permission to move the deep emotions of pain and confusion that would have brought me peace and understanding. There was no acceptance coming to me from outer reality, no fairy godmother in a neighbor, a grandmother, or an aunt that would hear me out and share wisdom to soothe my soul. I had to hold it and for me, the back of my mind became the dumping ground for everything I was ill equipped to handle. All of those feelings hid in the dark, outside my awareness and outside God's light, filling my emotional body, twisting my mind, and diminishing my light. Denial is a dark and lonely road. I went from a bright beautiful child to a teenager using drugs to self-medicate and as a means of escape. My confused, ungrounded nature brought into my reality suffering and injury from a motorcycle accident. This accident sent me whirling into the abyss of drug addiction and two near-death experiences due to accidental overdose. Some would say the accident should have been enough to wake me up. It did, but only for a short while as I was overwhelmed and the deep patterns of denial soon came into play. With nearly all my receptor sites filled with denial, fear, confusion, and pain, I had little room within me for the understandings that would have guided me out of the dark and into the light. At that time, I had yet to discover help in the form of a friend or facilitator. I had neither courage enough nor love enough for my own life to seek help and did not yet know how to help myself. I still had not allowed myself to feel what needed to be felt. I chose to drug myself, numb my feelings, my pain, and distract myself from everything that was attempting liberation. Feeling honest feelings was too tall an order at the time; one I did not realize would have started the process of setting me free.

Perhaps I am part of the slow learning group. I am at peace with that because I am alive and I am well equipped to share what I have learned on this long, dark road with you now. I did read many books but my growth and shift of energy is not because I read. I have had direct experiences through the process of applying what resonated with me step-by-step. I have felt what I could not feel and I have freed myself to such a degree that my life reflects the beauty that it was always meant to. It is from this knowing and trusting part of me that I share with you now. If you are just beginning this journey and are now aware of things you do not like in yourself, your life or the choices you have made, I urge you, do not beat yourself up further for what you did not know before. It simply slows the process. What you did not know, you did not know. What you are about to discover is the light at the end of the tunnel. If you have been on the path for some time and have found little change, persevere.

You may find it is time to dig a little deeper, get more involved in your life and the transformation of your energy. Perseverance will be your great asset. There is no turning back. As Oliver Wendell Holmes put it, "Man's mind, once stretched by a new idea, never regains its original dimension." You are a beautiful being, a spark of the Divine made manifest. That is something to celebrate. You can begin now.

What Happens to Denied Expression

Denying anything does not put an end to it. Denial disconnects what we are denying from the understandings needed to free us from the vibration and all that it attracts, which is why healthy change will not occur in a state of denial. Denial must be recognized for it to end and it must be let go of. It cannot let go on its own. It is held in place by the judgments that we have created and emotional control.

Let us use fear as an example. Denying the fear only disconnects the fear from our consciousness and the understandings that would free us from this fear. The fear is not gone but temporarily out of sight and out of mind, out of the light and held in the dark. A vibrational match for this fear will, sooner or later, present itself as the magnetic attractive energy of this fear draws the experience to us, not for the purpose of causing harm but for the sole purpose of liberating itself. An example might be, "I am afraid of heights." The truth is, "When I was young, I fell out of a tree and broke my arm. That frightened me and I have not released all the fear." Now the fear rises up for liberation every time there is an experience with height. What most people do is continue to limit the experience and repress the fear. To talk about being afraid of heights is not feeling the fear that has been held. The judgment "I am afraid of heights" is further strengthened by the emotional control of the unexpressed fear. The full expression of the fear relating to the singular event of falling out of the tree was denied likely due to the child being overwhelmed by the incident and all the subsequent events such as going to the hospital and well-meaning advice like "Be strong, don't cry," "Show us what a big boy you are," "Show us how tough you are." Without full expression, the energy of fear cannot evolve beyond the low-density vibration that is held unnoticed in a state of denial. When outer reality presents a situation for the purpose of liberating trapped energy, we can either release and liberate ourselves or amplify the energy, spinning in the drama, embracing the old pattern of judgment, trapping it in a state of denial, adding to the old emotional charge. Using this example, the person who is afraid of heights may come to a beautiful scenic overlook on a trip through the mountains. Once out of the car and at the edge of the lookout area, the person feeling the fear of heights begins to panic strengthening the judgment, "I am afraid of heights" and retreats from the lookout area and limits the experience. This would be spinning in the drama and again trapping the energy. Now doing it another way, the person feels the fear and begins to panic but realizes there is nothing to be afraid of and asks, "Why am I so afraid?" This person could breathe through the fear as it moves through and out of the body, reinforce the knowledge of safety and free a great deal of the trapped fear relating to heights. There is a likelihood the person may remember the tree incident as the light of understanding brings information to the conscious mind. Then the person puts it all together, liberating themselves from the old belief "I am afraid of heights."

Another example of a judgment holding fear in denial could be the idea that being afraid is weak. Release the judgment and emotional control allowing the fear to express itself, move out, and evolve into a higher vibration. The next time fear comes, it can be felt and understood for what it is rather than denied. Fear's true mission is to give us a reason to pause and reexamine something we are about to do or are doing and decide if the experience is right.

Feelings and Denial

Feelings are not to be dismissed or accepted in the way that an experience can be had or not. An experience is something outside of us. Feelings are a part of us and to deny feelings is to deny parts of ourselves. Any part of ourselves that we have denied must be brought back and accepted if we desire to be whole.

If we choose an experience over our feelings, the feelings do not disappear but wait for an opportunity to move, to express, to be accepted, and to evolve. Feelings are designed to inform us, not hold us back. True feelings can emerge and inform us when denial ends. If we do not have readiness for an experience, we reject the experience rather than accept the experience and reject the feelings about the experience. To accept an experience and not the feelings is the path of denial.

When emotions are overridden or denied because they are not liked, they are no longer allowed to remove us from the situations that we cannot accept or situations we are not ready for. After a painful experience we might ask ourselves, "How did I get into that situation?" If the Will were free and true feelings were allowed to express, we would have had internal guidance and information to make a better decision. Disconnected from true feelings, we can walk into situations that shock us. When feelings have been partially overridden, we have heard someone say, "I knew I wasn't supposed to be there, or I knew I should not have gone." That person felt the Will's response but ignored it. When the choice to deny feelings has been made denial, judgments, and other limiting conditions offer experiences of pain, confusion, disappointment, a sense of loss; all of which strengthen denial and judgments and further diminish personal power. When this goes on long enough, we will feel powerless and the role of victim becomes well defined in the life being led not lived. Denial of feelings can effectively break down the connection we have with our Spirit. This breakdown takes us further from the light of truth and deeper into the darkness of illusion and delusion, resulting in lost Will (personal power), lost vitality and health, lost hopes and dreams. When we embrace denial, we do not understand what is happening. With little light to expand our consciousness, we are simply in the dark.

The denied Will and broken connection to Spirit can also polarize to the role of tyrant rather than victim unleashing false Will (Will denied) disconnected from Heart and love of Spirit. With no love to guide or light to illuminate consciousness, a cruel and heartless component becomes the expression of the tyrant. Both victim and tyrant are out of balance. The vicious swing between tyrant and victim is evident in many people. For example, a manager treats an employee badly and that person does not standup to the manager. Then the person gets home and becomes the tyrant to members of the family that cannot or will stand up for themselves. This vicious cycle is a very difficult and confusing path but one that can be changed.

What Was Lost Must Now Be Found

To say things will never change is to align ourselves with denial. The feelings for change seem too overwhelming to accept. With this belief and the judgment created to support it, feelings are again denied and the path to freedom is out of sight and out of mind, empowering the false belief that nothing changes.

Once denial has crossed the midpoint, meaning we have denied half of ourselves or more, our magnetic center is weaker than the magnetic power of denial. This means the power to attract is given over to the denial. The expression of the Will becomes the expression of a false Will. A good honest question to ask ourselves is, "What am I attracting and what am I attracted to?" If we are attracting what we do not want, we are experiencing denial attracting more of itself.

Basic Guideline to inspire freedom from denial

Contemplate this:
If denial is denied, it cannot end.
If it does not end, it does not move.
If it does not move, the energy becomes denser.
The denser the energy becomes the more it attracts denial.

The denser our energy is the more difficult it is to manifest our desires. If the magnetic power of denial is stronger than our magnetic center, we will be manifesting our denials and this can happen with great speed. This is creating by default. Common questions that often accompany such personal creations are, "Why does this always happen to me?" or "Why do I attract losers, liars, or thieves?" Denial attracting more of itself is a vicious cycle but one that can be broken. When we begin with the intention of ending denial in our lives, events, and circumstances begin to shift in support of the intention. A shift of perception begins to illuminate denials so we can recognize them. Herein lies our opportunity to take that one important step. Look at what life is presenting. The opportunity to see more may come in the form of a person, circumstance, or situation. Stop, look, listen, and feel. Recognition is the first necessary step. Remember we have the power of choice step-by-step, minute-by-minute, and day-by-day.

Emotional Freedom and Free Will

Emotions are the expression of our Will. The Will desires to break free from the shackles of denial and desires to become useful, contributing fully in the expression and manifestation of life. Overpower the Will enough and a complete disconnect from Spirit will occur. Here are some examples of living life when the Will and the Spirit, the masculine/feminine aspects, are disconnected from one another.

When Spirit denies Will, we experience a loss of right-place/right-time. Presupposed time and schedules, calendars, and dates are adhered to since the Will is deactivated and lost through denial. The Spirit presses on, under stressful conditions, without regard to what is happening to the body, the mind, and the emotions. Spirit presence has no selection process because the function of the Will is to respond (through feelings) and select what feels best. When the Will denies Spirit, the magnetic force has no understanding of what it is attracting and why. Divine inspiration is lost when the Will has no acceptance for its own Spirit. This lack of acceptance gives way to expression of a false Will and misunderstanding. The experiences and chaos of living life disconnected from Spirit confuses us and we wonder why events and circumstances are happening to us, unaware of the significant role we have in creating it.

We must bring our thoughts and our feelings together. This coming together clears the way to receive communication from God directly. God can and does communicate with us directly, if we are receptive and open. If we are challenged to hear from God directly, there are many guides and angels that are happy to help us with deeper understanding and spiritual growth. The Divine gifts of intuition and communing with God directly or with our guides, and angels are not given to a few special people. This gift is available for all who are open to receive and feel Divine inspiration, guidance, and love.

Mother/Father God dwell within us. A heart that is dark and contracted by fear, doubt, judgment, and denial offers little room for the expression of love from the Divine. We must look into our hearts and ask, "Have I made room for my Divine Parents?" A heart that is open to the true nature of our being and the mystery of life, filled with light, expressing love, feeling truthfully, and ever evolving is where we will find God and the Divine Mother expressing through us with Grace. This is being attuned to our true Source. We need not take energy from anyone or be drained by others. Energy is flowing in great abundance when we are aligned with the Divine and whole within ourselves. For this to happen, denial must end. For denial to end, we must accept all of ourselves as we are right now.

Go To Bonus Media Center at:
http://www.ConsciousMastery.org/BonusMedia
To Download Bonus Media for Chapter Seven

I Recognize My Denial

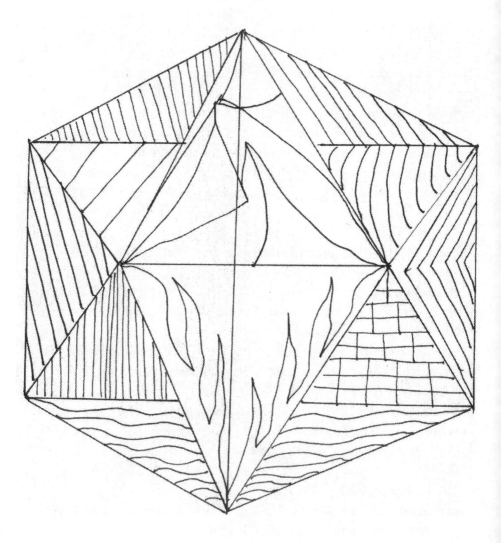

CHAPTER EIGHT

DENIAL PART TWO - RECOGNITION AND POSITIVE AFFIRMATIONS

Recognition, the First Step to Freedom

The energy lost in a state of denial constitutes much of the shadows within our beings but denial is not just about painful emotions unfelt. Denial will keep the light from everything. The recovery of hopes, dreams, talents and desires is one of the rewards for ending this difficult path. We are always creating our lives. Some are mastering the art of creating everything we do not want. This is creating by default, where denial is attracting more of itself. I am offering a way to create consciously. Master the ability to expand consciousness through the fluid expression of love and truth with the light of divine inspiration and expression of true feelings.

Denial is dense and does not move out on its own. We will have to do the work of recognizing our own denial. We must open our minds beyond the limiting structure of judgment. We must free emotional energy held in the emotional body. It is essential that we open our hearts, allowing heart essence to expand with the light of love and the liberated vibration of true feelings. The reward for a dedication to being the love we are is becoming the love we have always been.

The heart is the growing ground for balancing our energy with love and acceptance.

If the state of denial becomes extremely dense and heavy we can even deny denial. Eventually, the body also becomes affected by this heavy vibration and is reflected back to us in the form of ill health and accidents. This is a difficult and twisted road because recognition is vital if denial is to be seen for what it is. Once denial is recognized and accepted for what it is it can be dismantled. Space opens up for light to illuminate the process of transformation, recovering personal power, and balance. In this flow of energy, we discover Source has been waiting for us all along, to open and receive the endless supply of love. Liberating ourselves is not about reliving painful experiences. It is about releasing the pain. Denial holds transformation at bay. It is disconnected from any understanding. This is why recognition is the first important step. One small bit of recognition leads to another. This leads to acceptance bringing this heavy weight to an end. Freedom can and will be reclaimed.

Take the First Step

Be interested or choose to get interested in your own wholeness, your own transformation and healing. Why? Because energy that could be to your benefit begins to work against you, drawing the reflection of whatever you have denied or are denying into your outer reality. Begin the practice of recognizing every feeling and thought you would otherwise push away or ignore. Accept that it exists within you and if it does not serve you, consciously release it. If it is a debilitating thought, consciously replace it with a more loving thought. The old way of pushing it down, pretending it is not in you, and ignoring it is the path of denial. Take a look around you. What do you really see? How do you feel about your body, your life, and your relationships? No rose colored glasses, no turning a blind eye to anything, no matter how big or small. Do not fight what you see by making excuses, embellishing judgments, blaming others or denying what you know or sense to be so. The fight only strengthens denial. Conditions to love come in the forms of excuses, guilt, and judgment. Let yourself off the hook and begin to feel. Know that you are relieving yourself of a great burden. Through recognition and acceptance, you begin to understand what patterns are running your life. Look around you, look at yourself, and look within. Recognize and accept the major role you have in creating your life. If you do not like what you see remember: you created this therefore you can create something else.

When you decide to undertake the process of transforming your energy, great strides will be made in discovering the denials and judgments that have been weighing heavy in your life. The journey of recognition and acceptance will open space within for light to illuminate our thoughts and lighten up our energy field. With the light of God illuminating your consciousness, you become aware that you are loved and have always been loved.

Denial and Positive Affirmations

A great way to open the mind and free ourselves from the limited consciousness of denial, judgment, and guilt is through the use of positive affirmations. The light that comes with high vibrating thoughts lifts the spirit as the mind expands, embracing new territory of consciousness. There is often a feel-good response when beginning this practice. Positive thinking brings with it feelings of hope and energy. The mind opens to receive the nourishment given in abundance by the light of the Divine.

Positive affirmations were introduced into the mainstream many years ago, long enough for some to say it does not work. My first encounter with positive thinking was in the early 1970s with a book by Dr. Norman Vincent Peale called *"The Power of Positive Thinking."* This material made me aware of how deeply negative my thinking was and how often I belittled myself. It did not matter that I had a smile on my face, what mattered was how I felt and what I thought about myself. My life reflected this truth. After many years of positive thinking, this is what I discovered: to practice positive thinking or affirmations without honoring all our feelings is denying a part of ourselves. We strengthen one part with the positive affirmation and deny other parts. This is the reason much of the current positive affirmation methods result in reversals. When this happens, we feel as if the affirmation is not working when in fact it is working very well. Feelings and desires thought to be disciplined out of the self will begin to stir. Affirmations quicken the process.

When we are using positive affirmations, energy in opposition to the affirmation will begin calling for our attention to be liberated. If we deny this energy by burying it beneath more positive affirmations, we will become tired because we are consciously or unconsciously engaging in a struggle. The struggle strengthens the denied energy because of our increased rejection and continued refusal to accept this part of ourselves. Honor the whole practice of positive affirmations by allowing the energy to move freely. This is not about engaging in the negative dialogue, it is all about freeing trapped energy that is lodged within our emotional body affecting our physical and mental bodies as well.

Honoring the full scope of positive affirmations is honoring the release of trapped emotional energy and making use of healthy, life-affirming thoughts. This foundation of higher thinking is there for us to draw from as the process of releasing trapped energy begins in earnest. The flow of repressed energy will rise in vibration quicker if we direct our thoughts to align with higher consciousness.

Using Positive Affirmations

Ride on this wave of newly liberated energy into the light of greater awareness. Spinning in the drama and amplifying negative dialogue is counterproductive and harmful. If you find yourself moving in that direction, stop! Speak a loving, feel-good thought out loud. This will assist in commanding the energy to rise up. Feel the lift. Continue to allow the energy to move in the direction you are choosing. Feel your grief and apply thoughts of hope. Now you are rising up to meet a more loving vibration.

Feelings will begin to stir with your intention to free yourself from the old ways that no longer work for you whether you are using positive affirmations or not. If you have intent to grow becoming more of who you really are, begin to notice more in all areas of your life. Pay attention to your thoughts and feelings. Notice what is being reflected to you from your outer reality. What kind of relationships do you have? How do you relate to your body? What is the status of your health; mentally, emotionally and physically? How do you feel about your family, your home, and your job? How do you feel about yourself? What is your initial response when things go array? What are your first thoughts when a challenge greets you unexpected or when you are expecting confrontation? These questions, when answered, will assist you in the process of noticing more. The more familiar you become with how your life is unfolding the easier it will be to create consciously. Life as it is now shows you what you have created. Life unfolding shows you what you are creating through your thoughts and emotions.

To use the affirmation " I love myself" is a good place to start. Those who would start here desire to truly love themselves and that is healthy. The other aspect of this step is that everything held within that is not a vibrational match for self-love will begin to move in an attempt to expand and become a match for self-love. The parts that vibrate self-loathing or a lack of self-acceptance that have been denied expression will begin to stir. My advice, let it move, cry if you need to, use your voice to tone or sing, write in your journal, dance, walk, run, do yoga, move your body, and free your voice. What ever comes into your awareness as a way to assist the movement allow it, let it move out, short of causing harm. Direct the wave of energy with your thoughts on the course you want to go. Set your compass pointing to self-love and light. You can feel your pain and still direct your thoughts to higher consciousness. You can cry out the vibration of self-hate and direct thoughts toward self-love and ask for more light. I have done this and it works. Energy is energy; once it starts moving, take off the label and let it move, taking you higher and in the direction you want to go. It is your responsibility to direct the flow. You can do this with healthy inner self-talk or speak it out loud. Use your positive affirmations. You can write healthy self-love messages and speak them into the air. You are not alone. Mother/Father God and your guides can hear you. I have made the mistake of releasing energy and spinning in the drama amplifying the old messages of self-hate and painful conversations of the past. This is not the way to liberation. To direct the wave of newly liberating energy with the same old hateful self-talk is to get caught in the drama and amplify the lie you are attempting to transform. This is harmful, irresponsible, and debilitating.

Always release your energy responsibly. Do not hurt anyone or yourself in the process. Find a safe place to release. Let the energy move so it may evolve and rise up to match the vibration of "I love myself." As you release the old emotional charge, some of which may have been long forgotten, call in more light so your passageway may be illuminated. You will receive understandings that will carry you further while softening your heart. This process will open space for light and love to vibrate more freely within you. When you have released old charge and called in light you have consciously made more room within you to love yourself. Take the time to integrate the new energy and feel the love that has found its way home to your heart. Write in your journal and care for yourself by hydrating your body, feed yourself light, healthy food and rest. Forgive yourself for holding all this heavy energy and allow your heart to expand in the forgiveness of self. If you are ready to forgive others, you may but always begin with yourself. It is forgiving the self for holding this energy that opens the door to understand how to forgive others. This may take time. You will know when you are ready. Always end releases with thoughts and feelings of gratitude, acceptance, and forgiveness. Acknowledge the love you have for yourself, your creator, and your life.

What Is Happening

When we empty ourselves of old emotional charge, we have more room for the higher vibration of self-love. Space must be opened up for light to do what light does; light expands. Transformation includes reclaiming what we have lost and denied. It includes letting go of false beliefs, judgment, and energy that is not ours but we accepted as our own. It includes bringing home to our hearts the lost and fragmented parts of us. Light expands our awareness and our consciousness. This prepares the ground for receiving and accepting messages of Divine origin, which assists us on the journey of evolving and becoming more of who we truly are. These messages are given in the form of inspiration, insight, shifts in perception, and deeper understanding. As our frequency rises, life will reflect this higher vibration of healthy self-love. We will feel deeper love for ourselves, our lives and for others, as well as feeling more deeply loved by others. This cycle of clearing happens many times. Each time we release trapped emotions, freeing more of our Will, we gain more of our personal power, deepen our connection with our Spirit and gain new perspective about who we are and what motivates us in our lives. If we are not receiving any new understandings, we need to dig deeper and honestly assess whether we have been getting caught in the drama rather than liberating ourselves from the old emotional charge. True release always brings new understandings. The time has come to attune ourselves with the Divine guidance available to us. The guidance system is free Will and free Spirit complementing each other with Heart to balance the flow of energy.

Go To Bonus Media Center at:
http://www.ConsciousMastery.org/BonusMedia
To Download Bonus Media for Chapter Eight

My Heart Grows

CHAPTER NINE

SELF-RIGHTEOUSNESS AND HEARTLESSNESS

The essence or nature of the heart is love and love always seeks balance. Hatred is the extreme polarization of a viewpoint with no common ground and no intention of seeking balance. Where there is hatred, there is heartlessness. Where there is heartlessness, there is a strong yet false sense of self-righteousness. There is a judgmental structure surrounding self-righteousness. The mental construct of judgment says, "I am right." This is held in place with the denied emotion of fear that feels, "I might be wrong." Self-righteousness, in all its judgment and repressed fear, increases the separation of opposing points of view. The judgment here is "only my point of view is right." The gap between polarized, opposing views contains the intense emotional charge of all things denied, including hatred and heartlessness. The blindness that occurs leaves both sides without the possibility of seeing any similarities. The disconnection of self from Source, the light of God, perpetuates the blindness, and makes new information difficult to receive. A softening or expansion of points of view is extremely difficult under these circumstances.

There can be great resistance to the flow of love and expansion of heart essence, yet this is the very thing that would bring about the transformation from heartlessness to heart essence. Blaming, hating, and embracing self-righteousness strengthens heartlessness, which is not recognized for what it is. When points of view are rigidly held, they become fixed and frozen in place. Many times there is little memory or no memory of how or why or when it began. Heartlessness is heavily denied with preference for the judgment of "I am right." We choose to hold onto the judgment of being right rather than open to the flow of love that would bring light to see things from differing points of view.

When we stand in self-proclaimed righteousness, denied fear is some of the energy that must move and evolve into a higher vibration to allow more of the truth to reveal itself. The movement creates an opening and an opportunity for love to flow. When we begin to realize that what we blame others for is a reflection of what is in us too, we are ready to clear ourselves of blaming anger, rage, and fear. Pointing a finger at another person begins to hold no interest. Forgiveness can begin the softening or expansion of a viewpoint that will start the process of healing the self. Allowing love to vibrate strongly within the heart brings heartlessness to an end.

Heartlessness and rage have a long history in relationship to humanity. If we feel a strong need to be right, we need to dive into what is driving us in such a way. When we discover we are holding fear, rage, and heartlessness we must not slow the process of transforming the energies with further judgment. We must not judge ourselves or others for being bad or wrong, it slows the process of liberating and expanding our hearts. The true mission is to release and transform heartlessness into heart essence. If the why reveals itself, it is for our growth. If it does not, it was not necessary for growth. Releasing what no longer serves us is the goal, not reliving or dramatizing the story. Focus on the mission at hand, which is to allow our hearts to expand with the light of love. Then we can allow the energy that we are holding to move. Heart essence begins to expand and as the heart grows, it becomes possible to see different points of view from a more loving perspective. When we know our truth, we also know there is no need to make others see as we do but rather give loving allowance for others to walk the path of their own choosing. Regain your Will's lost alignment and reconnect with your own Spirit. This reunion of your Will and your Spirit restores the connection with Source, Mother/Father God.

What Are We Saying?

Self-righteousness and hatred will likely reveal some level of self-hatred. It is a good practice to notice how often the words "I hate" come from our lips or pass through our minds. What are we hating and why? Is it a word that is used haphazardly, referring to all and sundry? I hate the weather; I hate my job; I hate that dress, that person. What are we really saying and projecting into our reality? What is within us that is being reflected back to us when we hate or feel righteous? It is in these very conditions that heartlessness is vibrating out into the world. Words have power and the more intensely words are spoken, the more intense the vibration. Recognize every opportunity to move heartlessness out, allowing heart essence to expand and vibrate at the rate of love as it was intended. We begin with paying attention to our inner and outer speech. As simple as this may sound, becoming responsible for our speech and our thoughts is foundational in the process of our evolution. Transformation requires us to look at what is truly being presented. Self-honesty provides an opportunity to face fears without overwhelm and creates a foundation for acceptance.

Blind fear or blind anger translate as not looking at what is being presented because we do not like it and have no acceptance for it. This allows no room for healing or transformational processes. It is also dangerous, destructive, and counterproductive. When anger presents as a response to being asked to look at what we do not want to see, fear is the driving force. There is a fear of feeling the level of anger or rage that must move. There is also the anger or rage at the fear of feeling intense anger or rage. In a state of non-acceptance, all these fears get twisted into something they are not and grow to become so much more than they really are.

In a fixed, immovable state of being, the magnetic forces of opposition become too strong for change to unfold with Grace. Blind rage is not transformative or healing. It is an endless cycle of blaming rage that grows bigger with no intent to heal or open for the light of love. When the judgment that I am right and you are wrong is strong, the battle for a point of view becomes heartless. It is as heartless and senseless as the battle for whose God is real. Where there is heavy blame, there is intense fear of being blamed. This sets into motion the fierce need to be right. If we are not right then we are wrong and the blame we projected onto others could be our own. This thinking and the strong magnetic attraction of denied fear and the judgment holding it in place makes change, growth, and evolution extremely difficult and for some, impossible.

When people are able to do things that are cruel we know heartlessness exists. An open and loving heart is incapable of cruelty. We can swing from cruel to overly kind, filled with shame and regret for what has happened, and yet take no action to see it for what it is. Intent to end the pattern of behavior requires us to address the energy consciously. It is difficult to admit that heartlessness is the reason the pattern continues to have presence and power to express. Unfortunately many parents swing from one side to the other in this way with their children, as do spouses with one another. To have some small desire for truth and more love in our lives can create an opening, setting the holding pattern into motion. Heartlessness that contains denial begins to vibrate, opening space for love and light. When the intent is to grow in love, the movement expands the contracted energy of heartlessness, giving birth to greater heart essence. Where there is heartlessness, no one wins, no one is happy, and misery abounds. A series of emotional swings from shame and blame, to fear and regret with no acceptance or understanding, drags us deeper into the darkness of heartlessness and rage.

Desire a Life Filled with Heart Essence

When consciously releasing pent-up energy (old charge), choose a place you feel safe and give yourself the necessary time to move the energy. Call in the light of God to illuminate your newly expanding consciousness with greater truth. Direct your thoughts toward your heartfelt desires such as peace, understanding, patience, or whatever would lift you out of the dark and into the light. Plant the seed of forgiveness. Allow forgiveness to begin the transformation process, touching places within the heart that have been separated from the Divine flow of love. Body movement and sound are safe and effective ways of working with trapped energy for vibrating out heartlessness so that heart essence may expand. Get creative, using either or both of these as methods for releasing. There has been enough suffering; let love in.

Vibrating consciousness and feelings give birth to creation. What we think and feel is how we create. Desire plays a vital role in our ability to do so. It is magnetic energy that draws and attracts the light of love. Without emotions and the ability to feel, there is no energy for desire. Without desire our vibration slows and eventually can no longer support life. When living life fully and creatively, desire is present. Desire is not lust. To deny our desires, judging desire as a low, base energy is to extinguish the flame of life. Desire for a goal infuses the goal with creative vibration. To lust for a goal is blind and unquenchable, typically motivated by greed, fear, and a false sense of power. Let us desire to know the truth; desire to feel the expansion only love can bring; desire the flame of passion and love to light our way. This illuminates the path and the truth. Lust grips and attaches feverishly to the outcome, motivated by any means to obtain the goal, regardless of others and health of the self. This is heartlessness in action. Desire in the purest sense is the magnetic energy of the Will that attracts the light. Without love there is heartlessness. Ignite the flame of passion for life and allow the heart to open, expand, and vibrate with love. In this way, hatred and heartlessness are no more.

The term heartbreak seems appropriate in so far as the heart must break free from the bondage of fear and heartlessness. What is breaking is the structure of seemingly immovable judgments, denial, and all the heavy energy that composes heartlessness. This opening is a gift. If heartbreak is seen for the opportunity that it is, forgiveness and heart essence will expand, bringing greater vitality and softness to life that only heart and love can give. Begin to be open to the desire for living life with joy, love, and kindness.

The voice of guilt can chide us into believing desire is sinful or wrong. Judgments against desire create a limited point of view, leaving little room for love and passion. This viewpoint has an effect on all aspects of desire and begins to extinguish the flame of passion in all areas of life. The choice to hold fear and limit the energy of desire within the confines of judgment slows down our vibration. Without desire, our vibration is diminished, reducing the magnetic energy necessary to create what we want. We are still creating but the results will be a mixed bag of our denials and hopes. What we are asking for is greater love and greater heart essence, not more ways to lower our vibration, making life difficult. Allow desire to lead you into pleasant experiences. It is possible to both feel good and be good. Goodness does not require suffering. We may suffer during the process of shedding old skins and releasing old charge, however, once we have relieved the self of the great burden of old baggage, life is better, brighter, and more meaningful. We must become current in our energy and stop dragging old charge and judgment into every new experience that comes to greet us. Align with Source, trust and follow your passion and desires.

In this way, life begins to reflect qualities that are creative, natural, and pure. This is not to say we will never feel frustration, sadness, disappointment, or anger. It is to say we will feel these emotions clearly and honestly when they arise for the situation that brought them. We will have the wisdom, courage, insight, and strength to communicate these feelings in a loving way. We will take ownership of our emotions rather than blame something outside ourselves for how we feel. Being current in our energy is how emotions can move quickly, imparting truth and understanding. It is not to say we will never feel fear. It is to say we will be open and receptive to what fear has to tell us. Is it a timely warning or a nudge to have us rethink a decision? There may be times that what we thought was fear was actually excitement.

Remaining open and receptive to feeling what needs to be felt brings important and useable information. Vibration holds information. As the vibration increases, new information will be given to us. This will be of great value to us for our own growth process. When our vibration is aligned with Source there is no room for hatred, heartlessness, and self-righteousness. The light made available by Source makes kindness, growth, and understanding a way of life. In this way of life, there is no need to control others or stand rigidly in self-righteousness. Shame, blame, guilt and denial hold no power to influence our decisions. Allow love to expand the heart and more of the truth will reveal itself. Any part of our heart that is hard and unresponsive must yield, expand, and soften. What is more important to us? Are we holding staunchly to a point of view, needing to be right or are we fluid, confident and open-minded? Are we being all that we are? We have seen heartlessness in action in ways large and small. Move heartlessness out and let love in. The time is now to learn to feel and know you can trust your heart.

"The heart has reasons that reason does not understand"
Jacques Benigne Bossuel

Go To Bonus Media Center at:
http://www.ConsciousMastery.org/BonusMedia
To Download Bonus Media for Chapter Nine

CHAPTER TEN

POWER OF THOUGHT

"As a man thinketh in his heart, so is he" Proverbs 23:7

"We are what we think. All that we are arises with our thoughts. With our thoughts, we make our world." Buddha

Thought is the foundation on which we create our life. If we look at what the human race has accomplished, we will see that we have torn the world and ourselves apart. The fear, judgments, guilt, and the denial we participate in obscure the voice of love and the Divine impulse of love-inspired thought. Thoughts and the emotions that fuel those thoughts, create a directing of power that is and has always been within us. However, the execution of this power has been unconscious for a very long time. As humanity awakens from a deep sleep, the realization that our thoughts and the emotions that empower thought is how we have been creating reality, begins to dawn. The more we look solely outside ourselves in an attempt to understand how and what we have created in life, the more confused we will become. At some point, everyone must look inward, quieting the mind and reducing external stimulation to hear the voice within. We are creating our lives with our thoughts and our emotions.

Do you know what thoughts originate from you and which ones are regurgitated from external sources, such as the media? Taking time to know what we are thinking is vital. Connecting to true feelings is essential. We can learn from outside sources yet there comes a time when we need to connect to our hearts and own thoughts. The time is now to become more conscious of all that passes through our minds and bodies via the river of thought and the ocean of emotion. From this conscious place, we can direct the energy by choosing what thoughts to give attention to. The ability to discern which thoughts are supportive and which ones are debilitating becomes ever clearer. With this clarity comes the ease of choosing the natural flow of higher life affirming, loving, and supportive thoughts. In turn, the vibration of love grows ever stronger.

Everything we think, we will come to feel and what we feel manifests in qualities in our lives. Contemplate beauty and love. Goodness, beauty, and love of life will solidify when they join the thought process. To understand a thought, it must be felt. Words can be twisted by undercurrents of energy, empty with little-to-no power or full and unified with the power to move mountains. It all depends upon the emotional nature and involvement in conjunction with the thought or spoken word. Thought gives birth to spoken words. Everything that transpires comes about as a deliberate act that was brought forth through thought and emotion. Become conscious of your thoughts. Become responsible for what you create in your life. Allow love to be the energy that directs your thoughts and actions.

Thought and the Spoken Word

Be specific. A vague generalization can give way to undercurrents of energy, which can mislead and cause confusion. If we feel the undercurrent with no understanding of what we are feeling, it brings on a sense of mistrust. If we are awake, aware, and personally empowered, we will feel the undercurrents and will likely ask for greater clarity. Grow in the awareness of your inner dialogue as well as your daily conversations with other people. Herein lies much information about the vast love and understanding we embody, or conversely the judgments, limitations, and denial we may be carrying. Listen to yourself. We are not our over-active, chattering mind. We are so much more. We have the power to speak truthfully and kindly. We have within us the ability to direct our energy consciously as a whole heart-centered being, not just a thinking head.

"To a mind that is still, the whole universe surrenders." Chang Tzu

Absorbing the Thought Patterns of Others

Spoken words that did not originate in our own minds can and do affect our brains. This is important to know and it happens more often than we would imagine. A good example of this would be songs with lyrics listened to repeatedly. If we listen to music with degrading messages and content, it will have a detrimental effect on the nature and vibration of our thoughts. The same is true with repeated conversations and conversational themes of movies, TV shows, and the news. When we listen to and engage in gossip, this conversation style has a low vibration and has a negative effect on our state of being. Some groups use certain language over and over. If the language is life-enhancing, the effect will be up lifting, if it is vulgar it will not be. The same is true when we choose music to lift the spirit or soothe the soul. The desired results are felt because the frequency of the chosen music will lift the vibratory pattern of the listener. Become conscious of the choices we make. Become aware of how environment plays a role in the way we think and feel. Our environment includes our homes, work places, other people, as well as the places or things we choose for entertainment. A regular date with nature helps sort out negativity. Nature brings freshness to stale thoughts and lifts low vibrations brought on by some environments and social and family pressures.

High Frequency Thought Forms

The higher we vibrate, the easier it becomes to change our form. This includes the form reflected in the condition of our physical bodies, as well as thought forms, and the form reflected in our emotional bodies. For love to manifest, form and essence must come into alignment with Source. All aspects must be accepted and vibrate within the light of love. Divine impulse is an intrinsic marriage of inspired thought with truthful feelings. In this way, we are stepping up our frequency and stepping into the light of our own divinity becoming conscious creators in our own lives. A singular life has an effect on the whole of life. That translates to the importance of everyone as individuals and collectively as a community, society, and the whole human race.

What Are We Thinking?

Remember that every physical thing, whether for us or against us, was a sustained thought before it was a thing. Thought is creative action and always takes a physical form. Therefore, the thoughts we dwell upon become the things we have or do not have, including experiences we have or do not have. The tendency to have many thoughts and feelings moving through our bodies and minds with no awareness of what they are, leads us to shock and confusion about what life is presenting.

Much of humanity is spending many of its days disturbed. A disturbed mind has little peace and even less clarity. It is much like a muddy pond or a raging river. This is not a good place to create our following days or years. It is beneficial to meditate, gently slowing the rate at which our thoughts move through our mental landscapes. If we have too many thoughts, too quickly then too much goes by unnoticed. Meditation brings us closer to the here and now. Meditation is not always sitting quietly; walking quietly, doing yoga, or riding a bike all have meditative qualities. Creative pursuits such as music, painting, cooking, sculpting, knitting, or poetry all have meditative qualities. In whatever way you quiet your mind, gently bring your attention to your breath. Still the mind and behold the wonders of life. Inspiration can reach us when the mind is open, peaceful, and receptive.

Where Are We?

Thoughts and thinking are often rooted in the past, the future or in distractions chosen consciously or unconsciously. Rarely do we have our mind collected in the present moment for the majority of our day. Learning from the past liberates us from the invisible weight it brings. However, many of us find we are trapped in the past and not free of it. The past is over when the lessons have been learned. We regain our personal power and we become the recipient of its greatest gift. This gift is a wellspring of wisdom, from which we can draw at any time. The past is no longer weary weight we once knew. It becomes the light we have longed for. Proceed out of the past consciously, with lessons learned, and we bring new things into our lives that surpass any experience before.

To think of the future has its merit. It is part of the way we create our future. It is wise to be clear about what we think and feel about the future, as it will eventually come to pass. Our future is largely dependant upon the level of emotional certainty involved in the thought process, as well as how determined the thought is. If the future looks bleak and daunting, we will meet our match in the most dominant frequency. In this case, the frequency of fear accompanying a bleak and daunting outlook will bring about the very same. If our thoughts and feelings about the future are bright and hopeful, we will again meet our match, this time walking into a high frequency future. If we are swinging back and forth between the two, we will create a very unpredictable future and increase the time it will take for anything to manifest.

It is important to leave thoughts of the future and return our thoughts to the present. We must trust that what we chose to create will find us open and receptive. We live a full life by being awake and aware of our current timeline and what is happening here and now. Each moment gives us an opportunity to think, feel, act or react. High frequency thoughts provide a foundation for us to act appropriately rather than react to circumstance or situations. If our thoughts are scurrying from the past to the future, the ability to respond appropriately to the present is not possible. We must be grounded in the present to be aware of what is happening.

If we are to spend time with thoughts of the future, we should do it with the awareness that we are creating our future. We must remember to guard our thoughts from including a flow in the opposite direction. Then return to the present moment and continue to create ever more robustly from the powerful position of Now. If we are thinking of the past, we must be aware of where we are and determine to allow the past to be the wellspring of wisdom it is intended to be. It is sad to see how fast we can let time slip away with little-to-no growth by simply being somewhere else in our thoughts for most of our days. If we trust our thought projections of the future or visualizations, we do not have to nurse them all day long. We can trust the process and enjoy our current lives to the fullest. After all, now is really all we have. One moment in time, strung together with the next, to make days and weeks. It is in feeling great joy and love in the present that magnetizes our future desires into our reality with speed and accuracy. Remain open for lovely surprises because the universe often delivers something better than our thoughts and desires. The higher our frequency in the present moment, the more quickly we meet our match and the sweeter the manifestation.

If We Think It, We Can Bring It

Our thoughts of anything establish its origin. The thought-form of the thing is already ours in the field of possibility as soon as we think of it. When we do visualizations or thought projections, we can let the energy collapse upon return to the present moment. Our vibration lowers and soon we are aligned with doubt or fear of failure. Some call this getting real. But collapsing our energy after we have taken time to visualize and send thought-projections into our desired future is like crafting a lovely boat only to poke holes in it before it is put in the water. This counterproductive activity vibrates at the rate of little faith and lack of trust. All of this translates into a low frequency match finding its way to us. We could say, "I knew the boat would sink" and still not realize we were the ones who poked the holes in the boat in the first place.

Know Your Thoughts

Get present enough to know your thoughts. Embrace enough Will to free yourself from old low vibrating patterns of lack and disease. In other words, wake up enough to see yourself putting holes in your own boat and then stop doing it. Recognition comes before transformation. You must see things for what they are and still not let your energy collapse into the same old patterns you are attempting to break. It does require inner strength and courage to rise above your problems while you are still in them, to be responsible and do what you know in your heart would bring the changes you desire. Well, I have news for you: you are strong; you are courageous; and you are divine. You simply have to decide to embrace your divinity and your personal power. One thought at a time directs your energy somewhere. Where are you directing your energy?

Meeting Our Match

The Divine Source, who feels and knows our most secret thoughts, can reproduce our thoughts in physical form. This is another way of deepening the understanding that we are a creator in our lives and what we create has everything to do with what we think and feel. What constitutes a vibratory match for us is seen in our outer reality. Objectively look at our relationships, our health, and so on. It is energy resonating perfectly. As we sow; so shall we reap. We have the freedom to choose what we will think and just what thoughts we will affirm. We also have the freedom to choose to be honest with our feelings and direct them ever higher on the waves of inspired thought. Knowing that outer reality is a reflection of our thought patterns, are your thought patterns life affirming or life denying?

Free Will is the freedom to feel honest feelings. Free Spirit is the freedom to choose our own thoughts. If we are slaves to old patterns of thought that no longer serve us, such as thoughts that are not truthful or that create feelings of inferiority or superiority, we have neither Free Spirit nor Free Will. When we choose to resist being responsible for our own thoughts, to give up personal power, we will resonate with the masses that create by default. Mass consciousness is very much aligned with fear consciousness. When no alternative is specified and our thoughts are random and debilitating, we will be the recipients of whatever constitutes a match.

Do you know your thoughts? If you do not, there is no better time than the present to become more aware of what you are thinking. Do you know what you desire? Have you thought about how you would like your life to unfold? If not, now is the time. Can you feel your desires as though they have already manifested? If not, give your feelings some room and time to expand and become one with your desired thoughts. You are capable of so much more than you give yourself credit for. Your every thought paves the way for your destiny and your every emotion creates the experiences you have in life. The nature of your thoughts and feelings are the nature of your experiences. Learn from the past and let it go. Take time to meditate or visualize with intent a wondrous future, then let it go. Move about your day, fully present, vibrating at a rate high enough in this very moment so that you can meet your match in the next moment bringing light to your heart and a smile to your face. Health and happiness are intrinsically linked.

Journey:

Travel the river of thought, no matter the size
To the ocean of thought, where you realize
Your love, your Self, your Source

In the wonder of life unfolding
Trust will find you emboldened
To live the dream you've been holding

Go To Bonus Media Center at:
http://www.ConsciousMastery.org/BonusMedia
To Download Bonus Media for Chapter Ten

CHAPTER ELEVEN

DENIAL PART THREE - THE END OF THE ROAD

Negative Energy and Darkness

Negative energy is one side of the magnetic polarity that composes our masculine/feminine nature. Its opposite is positive energy. Both polarities are necessary. The negative polarity is magnetic in nature as described in the chapter Our Soul and the Divine Mother. Many think the negative polarity is the darkness but it is not. The negative polarity is attuned to the Will, which is our receptive feminine and intuitive nature, our feelings, the Mother Principle of our being. The darkness can be nothing yet in this darkness can be anything. If a healthy, joyful free Will vibrates open space in the darkness that has nothing in it, the newly opened space will fill easily with the unconditional love and light of Spirit raising our vibration. This is expansion at its best. The faster the Will vibrates the more space opens and expands with the light of love, the more attuned we become with the Divine Spirit of God. When space has been opened and light enters we have those great epiphanies and can experience brilliance, peace, love, and understanding.

If the space that opens is filled with our repressed emotions, this tells us our denied Will has increased its vibration enough to free itself. Energy that was stuck is now in motion. Unless the release was done consciously, this movement often appears disruptive because the opening was created by an event in outer reality, a trigger. When denied Will vibrates strongly enough to open space in the dark that contains it (denied Will) the shadows must exit so light can enter. The magnetic power of denied Will essence has drawn an experience toward itself big enough to bring our attention to what we have denied. What we do with it determines whether we transform the energy or spin in the drama. If we allow the energy in motion (our emotions) freedom to move, directing our thoughts ever higher, we are transforming the energy and releasing a great burden. The sole purpose of liberating the shadow or denied Will is to evolve. As the energy rises up to vibrate at the frequency of love, it adds to our personal power. With intent to transform the repressed emotional energy, to change the denied Will into Free Will, balance will be found. Peace will be felt. The ability to express true feelings will be natural and easy. Joy will become us. Both the negative and positive polarities are essential for balance.

Vibrational Match

The vibration of denied Will is slow and the energy is very dense. When we deny feelings and experiences, we create a build up of negatively charged energy. Remember this energy is magnetic in nature. When the Will becomes desperate for release it will magnetically draw a vibrational match from outer reality toward itself to trigger a release. From the Will's perspective, the purpose is to regain freedom and vibrate at the rate of love and acceptance. If the imprisoned Will is vibrating anger in the darkness of denial, it will attract more situations involving anger for the purpose of releasing the anger. Too often people get into angry situations without any understanding or intent to understand. This does not liberate the energy. It amplifies it as we spin in the drama, feeling a strong need to be right rather than call in the light of love to show the truth and a better way.

Disruptive behavior is an attempt of the Will to regain its lost alignment with its own Spirit and with Source. Triggers can become some people's only avenue for releasing blockages, opening space and providing a way out of the bondage created by denial. This is the difficult route to take. As we become more conscious, we can release pent-up energy freeing our Will consciously, long before a trigger sets energy into motion. To ignore lessons to the point when the Will becomes desperate can create great upheaval in our lives. This can be felt in any number of ways, such as health crisis, financial loss, and relationship or family breakdown. Lack of acceptance is death to the Will, whose very presence in our life depends on acceptance and the expression of true feelings as opposed to feelings twisted by judgment, denial, and fear of the truth.

In the dark can be nothing or anything. If shadows are lurking in the darkness, they must move out. Once space is opened, whether through a triggered experience or by conscious clearing, the space must be filled. With the shadows set free on the wave of emotional expression, call in the light of God to fill this space so you may become increasingly aware and better able to understand how you create your reality. Light illuminates our perspective by giving us the opportunity to see more and become more aware. With that, we are better equipped to make choices that are life affirming rather than life denying. Herein lies the opportunity for the Will to regain its lost alignment, closing the gap between itself and Source. As we free our Will, we free ourselves and regain our God-given personal power.

Light and Love

Spirit is life; it is light, it is love. It is the positive, action-oriented polarity. If the light of our Spirit fills the space opened by our Will with conditions, it is a mixture of light and denial. When the space is filled with conditions we give some of our attention to doubt, fear, and lack. This newly opened space begins to contract once again as denial begins to reduce the vibratory power needed to create the change we seek. Our prayers and desires require us to trust in our ability to create. In trusting our ability and the Laws of the Universe, we do our part by holding the space open unconditionally with patience and trust in the light of love. When denial is all that fills the space, the space closes, becomes heavy suppressing emotions once again. The opportunity to lighten up is missed. This is what happens when we spin in the drama and continue to ignore the new understanding being given by the light of Spirit and the responsibility we have in creating our own life.

When the space is filled with unconditional love and acceptance, there is no room for denial. It is our unyielding faith, love, and acceptance that holds the space filled with light open long enough for our desires and prayers to manifest. They are no longer fragmented by denial. They are whole and united by our trust and belief in the power of love. Love must flow freely and unconditionally. No amount of pressure or forced action will make it so. The same is true for feelings. Our minds cannot tell us how to feel. Emotions must have unconditional acceptance to move and express as true feelings rather than altered and manipulated. Accept Thyself. Love Thyself.

Denial and Self-Deception

If we have denied aspects of ourselves, entertaining the notion we are doing ourselves or someone else a favor or perhaps that it is noble, we must think again. It is all an illusion that embraces self-deception. Anything we think we might gain by representing ourselves falsely will fall away; this includes jobs, position in community, as well as people. Anyone who would prefer us to deny ourselves in favor of them does not have our best interests at heart. If you do comply, you do not have your own best interest at heart either. People often make choices to misrepresent themselves or to become someone other than themselves to keep the peace, fit it, gain something, or in the hope that other people will like or love them more. How can anyone really know who we are if we are not ourselves? If by chance anyone does seem to love us more, whom do they really love? How long can we keep up the façade? When the walls come tumbling down, the deception will be revealed. What then? Self-deception, as a by-product of denial, can occur without our conscious awareness. However, our lives will reflect this self-deception. Here are some examples. We may find ourselves saying things that do not feel right to us in hope of getting a particular response. We find ourselves agreeing to do things we do not want to do because we will feel guilty if we did not do it or tell ourselves that there was no choice. We may find ourselves hooked into relationships that are unhealthy, yet entertain excuses of why we should stay therefore cannot seem to end them. We may do or not do things because of what others might think. We dress to impress or attract someone, yet is not our true nature. We are finding no real joy in the work we do and tell ourselves that we have no choice. We get angry when we hear that we do have a choice and prefer to argue the reason we do not. We do not know what our true feelings are and let others choose for us. When we talk, we sound like our mothers or fathers. A feeling of anxiety accompanies any idea of change or a feeling of anxiety has us looking for ways to numb it rather than look in it for the cause. We make ourselves small so another can be comfortable around us or larger than life compensating for insecurities. We are doing a great disservice to ourselves, to others, and the world at large. We are each enough. We are each enough regardless of where we are in life or what others may have told us. Where we are is where we begin to make changes. It cannot happen at any other place, change begins where we are right now. That, in itself, is a comforting thought.

If we become a shell, filled with pretense and false images, we are open to attack, manipulation, overpowering, and we will, at some point, experience a breakdown of every illusion we hold. The energy of unconditional love and light that holds space open for our desires to manifest is not stagnant. It is vibrating very quickly and flowing toward us all the time. Open to receive it. The alternative path of denial is unstable, heavy, unhappy, and unnecessary and always resonates a lack of self-acceptance. Our outer world is always informing us about the conditions of our own inner world. Make a list of each of what is light in your world and what is heavy and see for yourself.

Here is the beauty of accepting yourself unconditionally right now: Change becomes possible and preferable. No one can control or manipulate us when we accept all of ourselves without judgment. Imagine how wonderful it feels to stand up for yourself and have a sense of purpose. At this point, our purpose is to rediscover and uncover all that we are. Begin to love and accept yourself right now from where you are at this very moment. The decision to accept ourselves just as we are right now begins the journey home to our own heart centers. It is not to say we will like everything about who or what we have become but to say that we will accept it because this is the only avenue where change is possible. Fear of not being enough, and many more fears, will rise up for liberation, not to scare us into remaining the same. Evolving, transforming the energy into a higher vibration of self-love, is what gives us the power to be true to ourselves and true to others. If someone does not like us for who we are, so be it. It is far better to know who we are, love ourselves and attract others that love. Relationships built on false information and pretense either wither on the vine or explode into heartbreaking pieces. There is nothing from Source that sustains relationships built on denial. Remember, denial is outside the light of God, where understanding, insight, hope, truth, and love pulsate. Love is there but we are not letting love in. The responsibility of being all that we are lies upon our shoulders. The same is true for everyone. We cannot do the work for others and they cannot do it for us. There is much freedom in knowing we are indeed creating our lives. Embrace the responsibility to do the work and support will find you. All that walk the path of truth find support and love, often in unexpected places and from unexpected people. The magic of life unfolds, delivering more of what we intend and desire. Let it be intent to be free from denial and be the desire to walk the path of love and wisdom. All our dreams and desires will find us.

Surround Yourself With Those Who Support Your New Growth

If we truly intend to create the life we deserve and desire but find that we are surrounded by people who do not support us, we must bring some distance between ourselves, the situation and those involved in order to continue to grow, gaining new and clear perspective. This may be accomplished taking these small yet powerful steps: make sure you take time to yourself, do not allow the negative talk of others to swim in your mind, spend more time in nature and places that feel good to you. It is also a good idea to keep a journal. Write your new thoughts and perspectives down rather than sharing them too soon with those that may feel uncomfortable or threatened by your growth. As our awareness of the truth begins to expand, our thoughts and feelings about what works for us and what does not will change. Those fearful, and therefore opposing our new growth, can be family, friends, or coworkers. The energy they deliver could be strong enough, when applied consistently, to break the momentum for change if we give our attention to it.

People who say they love and care about us can dampen our spirit for change. Often times their agenda for keeping us the same is more about them than it is about us. Their fear of change and the idea of what might happen or be lost to them if we change could be strong enough for them to decide, consciously or unconsciously, to use manipulation and other unkind tactics to steal our wind from our sails. They wonder, if you grow and stand up for yourself, and speak your truth, what will that do to their lives? If they call you selfish for taking your life back, ask yourself, who is really being selfish, you or the ones that want you to be less than the real you so their life remains undisturbed? Love yourself enough to distance yourself from the opposition for a time. You will feel your personal power grow as you integrate and welcome home your liberated Will and Spirit. Take time for yourself. You deserve it. Then surround yourself with those who support the newly emerging you.

If you thought denial would protect you from harm or from feelings you do not want to have, you have been mistaken. In truth it is quite the opposite. Denial offers an overwhelming reality of oppression and compression. Every denied aspect of yourself that tugs at you for your attention and acceptance will be reflected in your life. An example might be, "I always attract people that are untrustworthy." A few questions you might bravely ask yourself are, "What am I not trusting in myself? How am I deceiving myself? What do I gain or lose by having this drama in my life? What do I gain or lose by being someone other than myself?" It is up to you to see denial for what it is and bring this downward spiral of illusion to an end. It is far easier to end denial than it is to live in it.

It would have been easier to be true to ourselves and honor our feelings from the beginning, but, sadly, many of us were not taught that or encouraged to be honest with our feelings. Many of us were taught skills such as polite avoidance, politically correct speech, not to cry, to be seen but not heard, or to tell people what they want to hear. We are also taught it is selfish to love ourselves and do what we truly want to do. These lessons are the perfect opening for those expecting you to do what they want you to do regardless of how it feels to you. Is it selfish to do as our Will and Spirit inspires and guides us to do? The time has come to break through the veils of illusions.

Whatever Has Been Rejected Must Be Accepted and Reclaimed

We must reclaim what we have lost, step-by-step. Lost hopes, dreams, health, personal power, and much more have been lost in the practice of denial, which widens the gap of separation between true Source and us. This means bringing everything denied out of the dark and into the light step-by-step, accepting all of ourselves. Allow repressed energy to move and evolve. Feeling what has not been felt happens sooner or later when denied Will transforms into free Will. This is not about reliving painful experiences; it is about releasing trapped energy. We can release a lot of old charge without attaching to the stories. This does not happen all in one giant movement. That would be too much for us to handle. For this reason, we can have smaller experiences until we have arrived at the core of the pattern. When you have fully released a particular belief or pattern, those experiences are no longer part of your reality.

Transforming energy does not occur in the mind alone. The mind cannot tell our feelings how to feel. Allow the emotions to move and responsibly direct your thoughts. Ask for the energy of Grace to assist in the process of releasing old charge. This gently strengthens us as we breakthrough. This does not require us to relive painful experiences. It does ask of us to feel without attaching to the drama, thereby liberating our Will and recovering our personal power and connection with the essence of our own Spirit and Mother/Father God. It is the movement and liberation of this energy that is the focus not reliving an old story. The release of pent-up emotions can occur without the story but will always bring home to heart the core of the lesson to be learned. It is remaining open for a greater understanding that is the purpose, not spinning in the drama. When release is done consciously rather than waiting for an experience to come and trigger it, we will be more apt to experience a breakthrough rather than a breakdown. The time has come to attract love and peace. The endless flow of the vibration of love is our birthright and our gift. It is our responsibility to open, receive, and allow this ever-flowing wellspring of love to flow not only through us, but to others as well. The place to begin is with ourselves. The time is now. You are a beautiful being and always have been. Step into the light consciously and see for yourself.

Denial of Desire

Desire also needs acceptance. Whatever we cannot accept is denied. Desire is the magnetic energy of the Will that attracts the light. Embrace your desire for life, giving rise to greater receptivity and acceptance for all your desires. Denial of desire is no different then any other denial. When held in a state of denial our desire has little-to-no vibratory power to open space and become manifest. When we make life-denying choices such as denying time for fun, recreation, family, denying ourselves healthy food, exercise, proper rest, healthy friendships, great love etc., we are in fact denying the desire to truly live. A desire to live fully brings with it the light and love that desire naturally magnetizes and attracts to itself. Do you think Mother

Goddess/Father God hope, expects or demands that we deny our desire for life and the wonders that are sure to expand from such a great and powerful attraction to the light of love?

There is no clear way for us or God to know what we would like our reality to be if true feelings are denied. Without the light to illuminate our consciousness, what is denied is outside of our own awareness. If we are not whole in our desire or ourselves, it does not matter what part of our request or prayer is answered, the other part is not. We need to come together and truly know ourselves, to feel what we desire; then right-time/right-place and right-action will come together. Move into full alignment with Source; leave nothing outside of God's light. There is nothing about any of us that is unacceptable in the heart of Mother/Father God. It is only we who reject and deny ourselves. It is up to us to turn this around. To live life to the fullest with true happiness and joy is the greatest way to say thank you to our Divine Parents. Begin by accepting yourself just as you are right now. There is no other place to begin.

Free Your Energy, Free Your Will, Free Yourself

If understandings are not received, and nothing has been learned, similar situations repeat over and over. We have heard people say, "Why does this always happen to me?" The release of old charge never happened but spinning in the story and the drama did.

To avoid this cycle of upheaval with no results, slow down during times of great challenge; get into your heart center. Remember this is an opportunity for self-discovery, to reconnect with your spirit and recover your personal power, not an obstacle to such. The heart center is much like the eye of the storm. The calm helps us see events more clearly. The understandings can reach us as our mind is also calmed in the heart center. A mind void of peace and the light of Mother/Father God is a dark and dangerous place from which to make decisions. Having all our attention drawn to the outer world is like hanging out on the fringes of a tornado. It is painful, confusing, frightening, and we feel out of control. We become overwhelmed which paves the way of poor choices, denial and other limited consciousness. The more our energy compresses, the greater the fear becomes. Love is squeezed out. So, slow down, stop, get into your heart center, breathe, call in the light and wait. The voice of guidance and understanding will come and when it does write it down so you do not forget. Opportunity and change are often accompanied by a plethora of distractions.

Releasing and liberating the Will is the path to personal freedom and personal power regained. Our feelings are powerful, and when aligned with the Divine, provide the information we need to make great choices as well as the personal power to implement them. Our Spirit inspires and our Will responds to that inspiration. When our Spirit and Will communicate with acceptance of one another, our feminine and masculine aspects unite and harmonize in love. It is then our internal God-given guidance system is turned on and operational. With the Will cleared of old charge it is easy for us to be kind. We find ourselves in the right place at the right time executing right action. We can feel it and we know it. Merging thought and feeling into one, renewed inspiration becomes constant.

Go To Bonus Media Center at:
http://www.ConsciousMastery.org/BonusMedia
To Download Bonus Media for Chapter Eleven

CHAPTER TWELVE

Judgment

"Everything that irritates us about others can lead us to an understanding of ourselves." Carl Jung

Judgment, by one definition, is the ability to make considered decisions or come to sensible conclusions. It is wise to have sound judgment regarding the choices we make. It is much like having healthy boundaries. However, the judgment I am speaking of here has to do with the limitations placed on an experience through the practice of denial. From this perspective, judgment is a false sense of feeling justified and correct.

To impose judgment brings an illusion of control to compensate for a lack of understanding and personal power. Judgments maintain and amplify the polarization of a single idea. It is an all or nothing, black or white way of viewing life's experiences and people. Holding immovable viewpoints does not allow for balance. This narrow view limits the very nature of expanding possibilities. Expanding possibilities is a true gift, offered to everyone, that is open and free from limiting beliefs and judgment. Every situation we encounter deserves the time and attention to be seen and felt for what it is. With energy flowing freely, good choices can be made in the light of truth

Judgment and Denial

"The more one judges, the less one loves." Honore de Balzac

All judgments exhibit a lack of acceptance of the truth, the self, and the experience. Lack of acceptance is the way of denial. As with all denial, much of the truth is hidden in the dark. The parts of the truth that are visible are then twisted to falsely prove the judgment. Without the light of Spirit and the free flow of true feelings, we walk this plane of existence unaware and blind to what is happening and why. When feelings are denied in favor of a judgment, the denied and controlled emotions add strength to the judgment. The more a judgment is repeated, the stronger the pattern becomes, attracting more of the same. There is a lack of honest emotional movement and acceptance given to the current situation when it is judged in advance to be the same as something from the past. When a judgment is rigidly held in place, personal power is given over to the judgment and denial. This limits the possibilities for right action because the present situation is only seen through the veil of illusion presented by the judgment.

This is easily seen in the realm of religious zealots. The judgment of "I am right and you are wrong" is strengthened by the fear and anger that is held. When the judgment is challenged or tested, destructive rage and fear erupt into aggressive hostility in the name of God and righteousness. The energy is expressed with great power, equal to the repressed anger and fear for the sole purpose of convincing others and themselves that they are right. This need to be right comes with a great price and satisfaction is never sustainably attained. The expression of repressed fear and anger has nothing to do with a desire to grow and understand. When judgments are being defended, the intent has everything to do with being right and nothing to do with seeking truth, harmony or balance. In this way, the denied and controlled emotions strengthen the judgment by both repressing the energy and then unleashing it as a weapon to prove the judgment right. Nothing is being released with the intention of transforming the energy into a higher, more loving vibration. This leaves no room for an experience to be what it is, or what it could be without the rigidly held structure of judgment. Judgments always place limitations on an experience. Furthermore, when life magnifies denial, it empowers the judgment to be seen as justified and points of view become exceedingly narrow. When pretense, judgment, and denial appear to be reality, we are, in a sense, trapped.

Judgments prevent change and set us up to repeat similar situations. When a judgment is seen for what it is, the mind becomes free of limiting beliefs and begins the process of freeing the emotions that were previously denied and controlled by the judgment. This presents an opportunity for us to learn the lesson and bring an end to attracting and repeating a painful pattern. Unconditional acceptance is the way to see things for what they are, instead of what we hope them to be. The art of practicing unconditional acceptance begins with the self. This is the powerful path of creating consciously. Creating by default, allowing unconscious patterns of behavior to lead the way, is painful, confusing, and debilitating.

When emotions that have been controlled and denied begin to move, the expression is out of balance. Without the understanding that this repressed energy has been building up pressure, the amplified expression falsely justifies the judgment. Guilt, shame, and blame join in to further weaken us when we attempt to free ourselves from the bondage of judgment and denial. If the lower frequency messages of blame, shame, and guilt capture our attention, it will prevent a true and liberating release, which would have transformed repressed emotions into a higher and lighter vibration. The ability to penetrate the essence, to get to the core cause, is stopped unless a sincere intent to clear falsehood, judgment, and denial has been established. A deep, sincere intent to clear ourselves of judgment, denial, and old charge will stimulate healthy self-love. We will also begin to attract loving support and the understandings necessary to break this debilitating cycle. When we become responsible for our growth and our energy the only thing we will lose is the illusion that separates us from true Source and our divine selves.

Judgments Are Out of Time

When an experience confuses our understanding and we feel a need to define the experience, a judgment is made. Judgments exist after an experience has occurred and continues to affect future experiences causing judgments to be outside of the current time line. Judgments are also handed down and accepted with no direct experience. The judgments of another, possibly handed down through family lineage or group belief systems, impose their point of view as truth. This has nothing to do with an experience in the current time line. The judgments and beliefs have been put in place by something that occurred in the past.

Because of a judgment formed in the past, the true expression of emotion is confined to what the judgment will allow. The true expression and guidance of the Will is given over to the judgment, which slows down the magnetic energy of our own Will. This is how some come to believe nothing changes. Holding this judgment will prove itself true, as nothing can change in a state of denial held in place by the limited consciousness of the judgment. The more a judgment is repeated, the deeper the pattern, the greater the conditioning until we can even come to deny that a judgment exists by believing it to be the truth. Judgments must be seen for what they are. Holding rigid patterns until we meet our match is the hard way to learn to flow with Divine energy. Breaking patterns with intense experiences are often heartbreaking, catastrophic, or devastating. Learning, experiencing, observing, and evaluation can take place in the light without judgment. A far more graceful journey of self-discovery is one that embraces a sincere and conscious intent to know the self and to know the truth.

Become Conscious of Judgment

The truth expands along with the consciousness. Embrace a desire to know the truth. Release the need to attach to ideas and outcomes, which result in fixed and rigid thought patterns.

Release the need to be right and step back for a moment to give room for the truth of any situation to rise up. Be conscious of when and how often you judge a situation or people based on past experience. Does the past experience have any relevance to what is currently being presented? Is old emotional charge attracting certain people and situations to you for the sole purpose of recognizing your judgment? If so, dig deeper within yourself before assuming the same posture of tyrant or victim, or blindly believing the judgment to be correct. Ask yourself some important questions and then quietly feel your way through to the answer. Try to experience the nuances of the current opportunity with an open heart, open mind, and a free flow of emotions that help us feel the truth and see the situation for what it is. This is practicing the art of becoming more conscious.

If we are attracting situations that have us saying things like, "this always happens to me," or, "I can't trust anyone," or, "all of these people are stupid or crooks," know that somewhere within us, we are creating the fulfillment of a belief or judgment. Our vibration never lies; it attracts a match. A match of this nature will cease to happen when we have learned what we need to learn, let go of what we are holding, and then open to higher vibrations, new thoughts, and new experiences. The gift of discernment will be our guiding light rather than old beliefs and judgments. If we become conscious of our thoughts and feelings and more conscious of the situation at hand, we will become clear about our choices and what healthy boundaries are for us. We will discover the judgments we are holding and begin to see how they only serve to limit us. We may even discover where and how they began, but this is less important than recognizing how they have played out in our lives. Becoming free of judgment provides an avenue for us to become more aware of our surroundings. Our ability to recognize people and situations for who and what they are will inspire confidence in our God-given internal guidance system. Recognition of judgment is a step toward personal freedom and transformation.

Compromise

"One of the truest tests of integrity is its blunt refusal to compromise." Chinua Achebe

Compromise comes before an experience and obstructs the unfolding expression of an experience. How can you know what you want to experience if it is compromised prior to the experience? The judgment is against the full expression of the experience in advance. Make a note of how often you compromise an experience; take into account big and small compromises alike. Small consistent compromises, which are not aligned with the truth of who you are, become large pockets of repressed emotions. When you begin to become more conscious of how often you compromise an experience, you will begin to recognize the judgment that is motivating the compromise. Pay attention to the excuses that accompany many of the compromises you make. You will become more aware of how you feel about compromises and the judgment. Some compromises may truly feel good; others may not. Some may feel like you are selling yourself short. Others may have you discovering it has become a habit that offers an easy way to fit in, make peace, or give up on what you want to experience. The next discovery will be whether or not you truly know what you want. Judgments and compromise can erode our true inner sense of what we desire. This is a conscious exercise that can be done as you move through your day-to-day life. I recommend writing discoveries in a journal; again a journal becomes a road map of the inner landscape. This awareness brings light to what happens in daily life. What was previously unconscious becomes conscious paving a way for new and better choices that are current. When we are able to evaluate circumstances and events according to what is really happening in the present, we will experience the present moment. Being here, now, is a powerful place to be.

Judgments Falsely Prove Themselves Right

Anything that is severely out of balance, that moves or attempts to move, toward balance is judged because the initial expressions are out of balance. When an experience brings opportunity for trapped energy to move, we are not expressing emotions for the current situation alone. A backlog of repressed energy is also attempting liberation and evolution, hence, the imbalance.

An example of a judgment might be "anger is bad and brings trouble." The judgment that grows from that limits the experience and the ability to express truthfully whenever anger is involved. Hidden fear is also held so both anger and fear hold this judgment in place, giving it strength. If we are angry, and the anger is repressed for fear of the trouble it will cause, the action or conversation that follows will be less than honest. The judgment limits the experience, the truth, and the expression. If someone is angry with us, we may shrink from the experience in fear and miss the opportunity to clear the air and discover what caused the anger. There can be no understanding gained when denial is present and judgment is held rigidly in place. What does take place is misunderstanding, manipulation, and a continued loss of personal power.

Held anger draws to itself a vibrational match and when we hold anger, we will see anger in many seemingly unexplainable ways. We will be the one to get the angry store clerk or angry driver passing us with horn blowing and fist raised. We are confused because in our minds, we have not done anything wrong. Repressed anger creates an undercurrent of energy that attracts its own vibration. The match is made, and the anger attracts more of itself in the form of people, situations and circumstances. We can only hold so much anger. Sooner or later, a situation will come along that triggers repressed anger and it will most likely express in an out of balance state which then seems to prove that anger is bad and causes trouble. However, this is false information. Once the anger has been given acceptance and releasing old charge has completed, a state of balance comes into view. The judgment must be seen for what it is in order for this cycle to end. When the individual recognizes the judgment and comes to realize that anger is an emotion that can be expressed without causing trouble, feelings can begin to flow freely and honestly. The pattern of attracting angry people and situations over and over will come to an end when the judgment has been released, a new perspective dawns, and the repressed energy is free to evolve. As the process unfolds the light of understanding guides us to achieve inner harmony. This does not mean that we will never be angry again but it does mean the anger will express appropriately. With the release of the judgment and emotional control, we can now respond to current circumstances without the fear and previously held judgment regarding anger. Being honest makes for healthy relationships and brings about a healthy sense of self and the ability to have healthy boundaries.

For true liberation and balance to occur, the release of old charge must be done responsibility and with respect. There is to be no harm done to any other person or to the self. If the release is reckless, producing harm, the voice of guilt steps in justifying the need to suppress the energy and the cycle of unhealthy patterns of denial continue. This is not the process of evolving. If we feel we have no safe place in which to release pent-up energy, releasing the fear of "no safe place" is where to begin.

Fear of having no safe place is not unusual. It often translates to being afraid of being on Earth and the loss of a sense of the right to be that accompanies lost innocence and lost personal power. This reflects a base or root chakra imbalance. Breath exercises can help you feel grounded and connected with your own physical body. Getting out in nature, dancing, singing and toning a sound offer easy ways to deepen our sense of connection with our physical bodies and Earth. Asking for assistance is always a good idea when we feel a need for a helping hand. Reach out to a trusted friend or find a facilitator who can assist if you do not feel ready to move your energy on your own. If the release is done with respect for all of life and with intent to clear old charge, great strides in transformation and healing take place. This is when our personal power has opportunity to develop, and become known and useful to us. Allowing our energy to flow is what brings us into alignment with Source. Holding and repressing our energy is what causes separation and great pain. Let go. Breathe. You will rise to meet a new day and it will feel good.

Judgment and Fear

Judgments are created and designed to justify emotional control. Fear of overwhelming emotion holds judgment in place creating a preference for pretense, denial, and the avoidance of truth. No situation can be seen for what it is in the limitation of judgment and denial. Lack of understanding breeds fear. The earnest intent to see things as they are makes a difference. If the intent is to understand what is happening in our lives and why we are having certain types of experiences, opportunities will emerge to support that. Do not let the opportunity that arrives to support your growth be seen through the old paradigm that sees only bad luck. Stop, breathe and look deeper.

One judgment many of us hold is that fear has nothing good to offer and is not useful. The build up of denied fear and its eventual out of balance expression make this judgment appear true. Fear is a useful guide when it expresses free from the weight of the past. It is moving to get our attention to take a better look at something we are moving toward, whether it is a person, place, or event. If a conscious or unconscious choice is made to deny fear, opportunities for growth will still come but the openness to understand them will be missing.

Behavior that is meant to show fearlessness is an attempt to shift attention away from the fear that is present but hidden. Anger is an expression many people use when it is really fear that lies at the core. Judgments regarding fear keep fear expressing in ways that are confusing because it is not seen for what it is. Fear and avoiding the responsibility we have for creating this life keep judgments in place. As long as judgment is in place, denial is present.

Judgment and the Will

"So many dreams at first seem impossible, then they seem improbable, and then when we summon our will they soon become inevitable." Christopher Reeve

Many judgments are held against the Will and the expression of emotions. Without a free flow of energy, personal power, understanding, and conscious awareness of the truth are diminished. Authorities and parents have judged it necessary to break the Will of children, and those perceived as subordinates, so that order may be maintained. This is more about control than it is about order. Free expression has been deemed unacceptable for so long that speaking politically correct and using polite avoidance (withholding pertinent information) is preferred and often encouraged. Speaking the truth is thought to raise eyebrows, rock the boat, or cause trouble. The irony of such beliefs is that not speaking our truth is what really causes problems.

A false sense of justification can produce blame in an unconscious state. We feel we are not blaming anyone or anything in the light of feeling justified. Blame outside the light of consciousness is expressed in a state of denial and held in place by the judgment that allows us to feel right when, in truth, our consciousness is limited by a false sense of righteousness. This is seen in many religious systems where there is the belief in one way of how to reach God and it is their way. It is also seen in the way humans hold judgment against one another due to race, socioeconomic levels or lack of education, and political beliefs. The light of God grows dim in judgments of any kind. It is easy to see how some are blinded by the judgments they hold when they embrace them as truths. Great unkindness spawns from this self-proclaimed righteousness with a formidable power fueled by false beliefs, illusion, false power (power not aligned with Source), and false Will (denied Will). Now imagine a free Will. Imagine the freedom and ease to speak your truth. Imagine living life as it was always intended. We are born to live life whole, happy, and free. Be the love you so desire. When we are free from within, it is not only possible, it is inevitable.

Return to Balance and Truth

The way to come into balance is to begin accepting all parts of ourselves and our experiences. This is not to say we are to accept bad experiences into our lives, it is to say that we must come to accept an experience that has occurred. A return to personal power brings with it the power of discernment and healthy boundaries. Step-by-step, we come closer to our own hearts. As we do, our thoughts begin to reflect hope and the truth about our right to live a joyful life. Acceptance brings an opening that allows for understanding to reach us. We begin to see and know so much more than we did before we began to soften with self-acceptance and self love. Remember, intent makes the difference. Begin with the intent to see what judgments you are holding. Feel what needs to be felt. When we face our fears, change becomes positive and life affirming.

Seeing our judgments and fears for what they are begins the process of dismantling denial and the old ways that limit our current experiences. Understandings come to guide us in the form of intuition and expanded insight. They can come through our dreams or in the form of other people. When these insightful knowings arrive, the best thing to do is follow the guidance. The light of inspiration and guidance given by Mother/Father God informs every person who has intent to see the truth and align with Source. We are all so deeply loved. Remain open. An alignment with Source insures the journey of evolving and freeing emotional energy continues with Grace. We begin to know the difference between the voice of our Spirit and Divine assistance and the voices of judgment, guilt, shame, denial, and all low vibrating thought forms. Adhering to the guidance of denial, judgment, and guilt is to remain small, weak, and powerless. Aligning with the love and heart of Source gives us strength, clarity, courage, hope, and everything we need to create the life we desire.

To make judgments against aspects of self such as rage, sexuality, fear, anger, etc., puts these aspects into a state of denial where there is no acceptance for them. Without acceptance these energies weigh heavy upon the body, mind, spirit and soul. Life reflects to us what we are holding. If we find ourselves judging others, we can use this awareness as an opportunity to ask ourselves, "What I am holding? What am I denying that is being reflected to me by this judgment or this experience? What is this experience attempting to tell me about myself?" If our intent is to release judgment, we will see it for what it is. We cannot turn away from any thought that may present a new, expanded awareness, whether we like what we are being presented with or not. The very moment we realize a debilitating judgmental thought, we must consciously release it, and allow ourselves to stay open and embrace new information. Feelings will begin to stir. Although this may frighten us, this is the next step on the path to freedom and liberation of the self. It cannot be done in the mind alone. For change to truly take place feelings must be felt and a shift in consciousness accepted. In this way, the release of judgment and the dismantling of denial begin. Many aspects of our lives may fall away if the very foundation of its existence was false or is outdated. When the trapped emotional energy is released, if we steer it in the direction of the heart, new thoughts and opportunities will present themselves. Expanding and aligning our consciousness with our original blue print is a path of liberation and freedom. It is awakening from a deep sleep. Expressing truth through honest feelings, a kind heart, and higher thinking becomes the natural flow of day-to-day life.

Judgments and the Negative Polarity

Negative energy is as much a part of the total creation as positive energy. The acceptance of the negative receptive yin polarity, by lovingly allowing the movement of emotions, opens space for light to illuminate consciousness, deepen understandings, receive higher learning, embrace greater self-acceptance, and expand the possibilities of life. When feelings are accepted and move as true emotions space is opened for more light. This includes all emotions. Joy can open space for greater joy; happiness can open space for a higher vibration of happiness. These are associated with positive energy due to the higher vibration. Anger can open space for light rising up and out of the lower frequency and into a higher vibration of peace and understanding. The judgment that negative energy is bad, that it must be controlled, and should not be expressed is due to the misunderstanding that the lower vibrations cannot be trusted, have nothing worthwhile to offer, or will cause conflict so a preference is made to only feeling good at any cost. A lack of trust and understanding for the expression of anger and fear is further justified when the repressed energy surfaces at a trigger. If we encounter a situation that brings up anger and our energy is current, clear of old charge, and flowing freely, the anger would be expressed appropriately and end very quickly.

The negative polarity is also associated with intuition, inner sensing, and insight. It informs us through the free flow of energy expressed as emotion. The low frequency band of the negative polarity such as fear, anger, or grief has every desire to inform us and evolve rising to a higher vibration as well. This cannot happen if the energy is not given the acceptance needed to express. Emotions express in an out of balance state when the essence of Spirit and essence of Will are not attuned to one another. This is when thoughts and feelings are not aligned with one another, not accepted for what they are, and not aligned with the Divine. The release of pent-up energy is always out of balance but is equally seeking balance. If allowed expression, balance will be restored. The degree of imbalance is proportional to the degree of separation between our Spirit and Will, and our lost connection with the Divine.

Judgment and the Mind

Thought forms attach to the thinker. Judgments and other limited patterns of thinking are held in the mental body; therefore, the mind has the power to release the limited thinking of the judgment. When the intent to see judgments for what they are is sincere, the mind opens and a greater truth is revealed. At this point, we have a great opportunity to feel, heal, and grow. Action must be taken to align with this new awareness by freeing the repressed emotions and allowing the mind to broaden beyond what was to a new state of what is and even further to what will be. Without responsible active participation, the opening, brought about by the intention or the trigger, closes once again. To continue resisting the opportunity to learn will bring an experience with enough intensity to break the pattern so release can occur. This is the difficult road and by no means the only way. Thoughts are very important, but this is not a mental process alone. The way to liberation must involve both thoughts and feelings. Free your mind, free your feelings, and free yourself so you may rise to a new way of expressing and enjoy the greatest gift given to us...life itself.

The Nature of Judgment Is Determined by Intent

If love and acceptance are present, the spirit of humanity is nonjudgmental. We must bring awareness to the deepest truth and that is intention. If we use words that do not sound judgmental but the energy driving the words have intent to judge, a judgment is limiting the energy. The more we clear ourselves of old emotional charge, the easier it is to discern undercurrents in ourselves and others. An undercurrent is a flow of energy and information that is not in alignment with what is being presented on the surface. When standing in the light of Source, it is clear to see there is no right place or right time to judge anyone or anything. It is however, right place and right time - here and now - to release and bring judgments to an end. Start with yourself. If you are to make any real changes in your life, it always begins with you. That is a very good thing because you are with you all day, every day.

Judge No One by What Is Right for You

"Teach not him who does not want to know." Ram Dass

No one knows the path of another or the timing of another's awakening. To impose a process of evolution upon one who is not interested, not ready or otherwise unwilling is to deny that person their right place and time. Our paths may be shared but not pushed upon another.

To communicate our growth in this way is to deny our inner knowing that we are imposing rather than sharing our view with another. Everything we are attempting to clear in ourselves will rise up to reflect this to us. Undoubtedly, we will meet with resistance from the other, just for starters. It will be up to us to feel it and see the truth. The best course of action with those not ready or choosing another path is to lovingly let them go their own way. Manipulating another to agree with our point of view will impede our progress and theirs. If we remain surrounded by those not ready to grow and unhappy about our newly emerging selves our progress will be obstructed. Herein lies an opportunity to love all that we are and find the strength to break free. This often includes a break away from some people. When we love ourselves unconditionally, we can truly love another unconditionally. As we grow and evolve, passion fuels our desire to truly know ourselves, embrace our strengths and live a life we truly love. We are worthy of great love. Deliberately intend to know thyself. If it means we are leaving an old life, releasing old judgments, and are putting an end to limiting our experiences then so much the better. Remember, our new lives are awaiting our arrival. We can see things for what they truly are and break free from the illusion. Everything we are is enough and everything we need to create the life we desire is within us. The driving force behind this is love. The source of the never-ending supply of love is our connection with Mother/Father God. We will find Source in our own heart center.

Honor Life and Truth

To honor all life and the truth that lies within is paramount to aligning with Mother/Father God. It becomes as simple as one thought at a time in the direction of honoring life and truth. As one thought leads to another, so does one action lead to another. The process is to direct thoughts one by one, no pressure to get somewhere, just letting one well-directed thought lead the way to the next, remaining fluid, no gripping, just flowing with the higher vibration of love and all the possibilities that present themselves in this wave of new awakening. When our hearts are available, open and filled with love, then our reality will reflect that love.

Formal Release of Judgment with Intent to Be Free

Start wherever you are. If you are unaware of any judgments you might be holding, but your life reflects unhappiness or scarcity, you could begin with a formal intent to be made aware of the judgments you are holding. An example could be: I release the veils that keep me blind and unaware of any judgment I am holding. I am now open to see what is keeping me in a limited reality I do not like. May the Grace of Mother/Father God be with me on this journey.

Continue to use this or a version that resonates with you until you become aware of the subtle energies that exist in the patterns of judgment and denial.

The Heart of the Matter

For the entire process, feel and hold the intention in the center of your being, your heart center. As the process unfolds, you may feel it in different parts of your body. Honor the feeling by bringing your attention to them. As the pent-up energy begins to move, these feelings will impart information that will help in both understanding and clearing the judgment and the emotions held by the judgment. As often as possible, return to your heart center. Breathe and call in the light of God to illuminate the process so true understanding will guide you safely. The intended outcome is a strong reconnection with the Divine, the true Source of love and wisdom and with that you will discover more of your true Self.

Things to Be Aware of When Releasing Judgment

In the process of releasing energy, it is vital that we not direct our anger or other dense energies at another person. This hurts them, and also hurts us. This is not evolving. It is amplifying the drama and pain we are attempting to free ourselves from. Energy transformation or healing occurs when the release is given to Mother/Father God to be requalified and we call it back to ourselves in the form of light. Energy is never destroyed, it simply changes form. What we are intending to do is transform the limited consciousness of judgment into high vibrating thought forms that reveal truth. We are liberating and transforming the trapped emotional energy from the low vibration of fear, anger, greed, guilt, etc., to higher vibrations expressing self-acceptance, peace, gratitude, love, and kindness.

When the transformation of energy has taken place it is important to care for ourselves and this new energy. We must be mindful of what is watched on television, on your computer, or movies. We need to be aware of what conversations we engage in. Remember, gossip is a poison and negative conversations lower our vibration. In essence, we should be mindful of what we feed our bodies and minds. Until all the energy has integrated and the new light that is shifting the vibration to a higher level has stabilized, remain quiet and introspective. It is important to take time to write new thoughts into a journal.

To speak too soon of new awareness with anyone can drain energy. If we share our experience in these early stages, we must use discernment and share with someone who is trusted and is happy for our growth. Even then, it may not be the best choice. I do not recommend it and it is not a replacement for journaling. A journal will provide great benefit for reviewing progress and the fresh new perspectives. It will allow denial to be seen for what it is. Recognition of denial is the beginning of the end for denial. This same release process can then be used for releasing denial. This means more personal power, greater self-acceptance and confidence, a greater capacity to love and be loved, expanded consciousness, and the ability to see life for the amazing adventure that it. This becomes the new reality.

It is important to honor the pause in the process and move into the relaxation portion. There is no benefit in pushing to release more energy than is ready to go. It becomes drama, playing and amplifying the energy, rather than release. This is counterproductive. There is Divine timing in everything. Knowing the difference between pushing to hard and going with the flow is another way the vibration of Grace comes to assist. As we do more conscious releases, we may find ways that are our own. Growth is one step at a time; some of these steps are giant steps. Conscious releasing with intent to transform energy and align with the truth is a giant step.

Go To Bonus Media Center at:
http://www.ConsciousMastery.org/BonusMedia
To Download Bonus Media for Chapter Twelve

CHAPTER THIRTEEN

GUILT AND THE POWER TO END ITS INFLUENCE

"Guilt is perhaps the most painful companion of death." Coco Chanel

Guilt, the unseen dictator, is affecting and infecting many lives. Guilt wields tremendous power and I wonder if people really understand how much of their power to make decisions is taken over by guilt. Many feel guilt keeps them in line, adopting the illusion that guilt provides a good conscience. If we are accepting all of ourselves and have an open and loving heart, there is no room for guilt and no need for it. Guilt has the power to suppress emotions and to strengthen judgments and denial when we listen to and believe the voice of guilt. Guilt destroys peace of mind. A lack of self-acceptance and healthy self-love is the gateway that leads to great suffering and disease. Denial, judgment, and guilt work in concert to diminish true power and hasten death, physical death and the death of dreams, hope, love, kindness, joy, happiness, and all that make living on Earth the journey it was intended to be. We must come to know the difference between love and guilt. The more we choose love free from guilt, the more things will move and shift in our inner world which is then reflected in our outer world.

Attention!

Guilt exists in part because we give it our attention. Giving our attention to the voice of guilt within and the guilt others have that they share provides the energy needed to manipulate us. Guilt succeeds in making us feel small, fearful, and powerless. Remember, energy flows where attention goes. The more attention given to guilt, the less power we have to live life by conscious design, which includes choosing wisely and taking action appropriately. Like denial, guilt comes into being wherever there is a lack of acceptance for ourselves. Guilt will vanish when we truly and totally accept ourselves for who we are. Let go and begin to flow in the direction that feels better. Energy begins to move as we allow our emotions to express with intent to align with love. The voice of guilt will become unmistakable when love makes its way into our thoughts and we will have no more of it. We will know the difference because we will feel it.

How We Recognize the Voice of Guilt

"Guilt is always jealous." John Ray

One way to distinguish the difference between healthy, constructive guidance and unhealthy criticism given by guilt is to feel if there is love in it. Guilt is a loveless energy and therefore has no love in the criticism it delivers. Whether it is in our own minds or comes from another, if guilt is the guide, it leads to self-doubt and pain. Guilt tells us it is unloving to have certain feelings. It is the voice that leads us to believe we should feel differently than we do. If guilt is accepted while our feelings are denied, we give our power to guilt. We have disempowered ourselves.

Some of the messages from guilt prey upon our fear of inadequacy, which stems from a lack of acceptance for the self. The false belief that we are not enough is one of the greatest lies we tell ourselves. It is sad to know that a vast number of human beings feel they are not good enough, young enough, old enough, tall enough, pretty enough, rich enough, smart enough and the list goes on. These beliefs run deep and are the cause of much suffering. I was one of these people and I know how debilitating it is to believe such falsehood. The truth is we are enough, but for those who will not or cannot embrace this truth, for them it just is not true. Life reflects what we believe it to be. What is believed, defines the truth. Do the beliefs you hold about yourself feel good to you? Do you believe you are enough? If not, experiment with the idea that you are enough and be willing to remind yourself of this daily. Check in with how you feel after a week of reminding yourself that you are a divine being experiencing life on Earth.

Sadly, the message of not enough is consciously and unconsciously transferred to us from people we trust to complete strangers in advertisement campaigns. When someone has a knack for making others feel guilty, it is because that person has guilt within and innately knows how guilt works. Guilt is a master in the art of deception and manipulation. Those who find it necessary to belittle and make others feel unworthy are themselves feeling worthless.

As Paramahansa Yogananda said, "If you want to be spiritual, seek good company and don't mix with those whose bad habits may wrongly influence you." Our environment includes the people in it. When we are young, we cannot choose our family, but as we grow to become responsible adults, we can choose how and with whom we spend our time and energy.

Oh, the Familiar Ring

"Guilt is the source of sorrow, 'tis the fiend, th' avenging fiend, that follows us behind with whips and strings." Nicholas Rowe

Guilt's voice can be convincing; it often sounds much like one of our parents. It has the ring of authority and gains power by capturing our attention. If we are dancing with guilt, we know well that it is a prison guard with but one prisoner to focus upon. Guilt knows the ins and outs of our worst nightmares, our best-kept secrets, and our forgotten pain. Our own perceived weakness is where the attack and capture begins, which is why the voice of guilt often appears to be speaking the truth. The attention given to guilt will make and keep us small and powerless. Guilt is also reflected back to us by other people through experiences that have no integrity, leading to disappointment or worse. Guilt appears in conversations that belittle and chide us into doing or saying things we did not want. Guilt takes the wind out of our sails when we are ready to make a difference in our own lives. Life will play out in a way that falsely proves the voice of guilt until we see if for what it is.

When guilt rules, our decision-making ability is given over to the unseen dictator. This loss of personal power erodes our ability to stand up for ourselves and speak our truth. We lose our way and can arrive at a place where we no longer know what our truth is or that we even have the ground under our feet to stand up for ourselves. Our right to be is lost. This adds to the confusion in identifying the voice of guilt and all the lies that come with it.

But remember this, if you feel no love in what you hear, turn your attention to a loving thought. Break the chain that binds you. Stop paying attention to the cycle of debilitating dialogue, whether it is in your own mind or comes from another person. Find one thought that leads you out of the dark. That first step will lead you to another more loving thought. One step at a time always takes you somewhere.

Guilt and Denial Walk Hand-in-Hand

Where there is a lack of self-acceptance there is denial; where there is denial there is guilt. Denial, guilt, and judgment are the heavy weights, the three powerful guards holding our truth, our Will, our light, and our personal power prisoner. They are only powerful because we have given over our personal power to them through the choices we made or did not make. Guilt speaks with great authority, guiding us to further deny our true feelings. Our souls know the truth, they feel it. Our hearts long to expand in love; we must think loving thoughts. It may be necessary to get angry at the voice of guilt and be forceful when changing the direction of our thoughts. We could say, "Enough is enough; I will not make any more decisions based on guilt. I am going to listen to my heart," and then bring our attention to our hearts.

Guilt says many of our emotions are not to be expressed because they are unloving or unkind and should be hidden or held back. Guilt guides us to lie to ourselves, to deny our true feelings, thereby disempower ourselves and mislead others. How absurd. Denying our feelings, whatever they may be, is unloving. Feelings bring information and in order for the information to be received, the feelings must be expressed. The difficulty in understanding this comes when old charge moves with current circumstances. It takes time to come into balance when emotions have been denied for so long. It is love and acceptance that will open space long enough for balance to be found. Guilt uses out of balanced expressions as proof that certain emotions are to be denied. Nothing could be further from the truth but when guilt has presence, it blocks the light of truth. The next vibration that guilt sends to the front of the line is shame. There is no love, forgiveness or kindness in shame; let it go.

Giving and Receiving in the Presence of Guilt

Guilt will never allow us to feel clear and comfortable when receiving or giving a gift, whether that gift is time, opportunity, a compliment, or a physical gift. On some level guilt will sound off, guiding us to believe it is not what it seems, it is never enough, or is wrong in some way. Gifts given with strings attached always lead to guilt because guilt puts the strings in place. These invisible strings come with hidden expectations of a return. When guilt is present, whether we are giving or receiving a gift, subtle, conflicting, and unsettling information is present. If our ability to discern the undercurrents is strong, we can ask clarifying questions. Questions that clarify the intent can be "This is very nice, thank you. Did you want something in return?" When we are standing in our personal power and the gift offering does not feel right, we can easily express the truth, "Thank you, however, I am uncomfortable with this offering. It would feel better for me to not accept this. I hope you understand." If we want something when offering a gift, we must be courageous enough to let the recipient know, "I would like to give you this and was hoping you had some time to spend with me. Perhaps we could get a cup of coffee?" Most people can feel undercurrents of energy but few bring it out in the open; instead of the exchange feeling purely joyous, grateful, and comfortable, guilt rides along as an undercurrent of low vibrating energy creating distrust and eroding the nature of giving and receiving from the heart.

Many people are comfortable with giving but uncomfortable with receiving, even something as simple as a compliment or a hug. This is out of balance. The ocean's tides flow in and out, this is natural. Our energy is designed to flow, to give and receive; this too is natural. If we are comfortable with the flow going only in one direction, this is not natural. What surfaces, sooner or later, with those that can only give, is deep pain and confusion about why they do not receive opportunities, acknowledgments, assistance, or material gains. For anything to come in, we must be open to receive. When someone attempts to give us something and we say, "Oh, that's ok," what we are really saying is, "I don't feel worthy and have no understanding of how to receive." The same is true for us when we only take, too lost and fearful to give anything back. It is not natural and, sooner or later, the emptiness sets in. No matter how much we have in material and earthly goods, the heart is empty. As in the words of Maya Angelou, "I've learned that you shouldn't go through life with a catcher's mitt on both hands; you need to be able to throw something back."

Guilt and Exhaustion

Guilt is the nagging voice reminding us of not having done enough, not having been enough and not being good enough. Guilt will find ways to influence us to do things that we do not want to do or does not feel right. When we override our feelings in favor of guilt, we fall victim to messages like, if you cared you would do this, if you were brave you would do that, if you loved me, you would do this. This can go on until we find ourselves agreeing more to what we do not want and less of what we do. This can confuse us to the point of not knowing what we want anymore because our true feelings are hidden behind the veil of denial. The power to decide should not be given over to the voice of guilt, whether the voice is in our own mind or is delivered by someone else.

Guilt keeps us pushing ourselves to do more, be more, and somehow we still feel unworthy. A lack of balance is reflected in the disregard for other parts of our lives such as family, friends, play, quiet time and our own health. Demand for endless sacrifice in the name of love is guilt parading as love, which is a common manipulating tool of guilt. But remember this, guilt is a loveless energy. It is a lie. The sacrifice is not for love it is for control. When guilt is dictating our lives, it acquires more of our essence, leaving us tired, confused, angry and disempowered. Guilt has control and often we do not recognize this invisible force that haunts us relentlessly.

Guilt and the Blame Game

"A man can fail many times, but he isn't a failure until he begins to blame somebody else." John Burroughs

Guilt can make us feel responsible for everything. Blame comes when we no longer want to feel that way. Feeling responsible for everything is a self-generated illusion that often excludes being responsible for our own happiness. In order to justify the imbalance, we blame circumstances and other people. Thinking, "I have to do this, I have no choice" is an example of unconscious blaming. This route typically leads to anger. Although anger could be a breakthrough, which could clear the air allowing us to see more clearly bringing an end to the imbalance, guilt will have most of us feeling guilty about the anger. Giving our attention to guilt creates a viscous cycle. In return for our attention, guilt deprives us of our personal power. This is not a good exchange of energy. The more we deny true feelings, the easier it is for guilt to lead our lives. A buildup of denied anger and blame will find a release sooner or later. By the time it finally expresses, it is often inappropriate in its timing and intensity. This then brings on shame, with the voice of guilt leaping in, securing attention with familiar negative self-talk.

The next unconscious stage is to fall victim to shame, move back and let guilt run the show again. The cycle of doing and giving more than we want and the illusion of being responsible for everything begins again. In these situations, what we are not being responsible for is our own happiness, which is the true responsibility of everyone living on Earth. The denied resentment and anger build under the surface and eventually leak out as blame. Sarcasm is a way many use to relieve the building pressure of anger. Here again the voice of guilt tells us that honest feelings are unloving and should not be expressed. What is truly unacceptable and unloving is living in a state of denial with guilt, judgment, and fear as our commanders in chief. We must be fully present, both in Spirit and Will, for any new understandings to be received and to take root. To be fully present, we must accept our lives and ourselves as they are right now. We will not like everything we are seeing and accepting but we must see and accept what is. From here change can begin.

The voice of guilt is filled with have to, should, and should not, as well as claims that it is the right thing to do, it is the responsible thing to do, it is the loving thing to do, even when much of us is in opposition to it. When we make a decision we cannot accept, guilt eats us up. A lack of acceptance for self and experience never leads to anything but pain and sorrow. Every aspect or part of ourselves that we do not love, that we do not accept, that we reject is a gateway for denial. Whatever we deny is where guilt will greet us. We need to take a good look around our world, our everyday lives; it is worth the time. The reward is freedom from the illusion of powerlessness.

A walk into our heartfelt personal power mends the relationship with ourselves and true Source so that love grows.

Inner Strength and Courage to Do It Differently

There are things we know in our hearts to be right, actions that require our time, attention, and energy. We know our bodies would love and appreciate a daily walk, yet we opt for snacks, dessert, or television instead. We say things like, "I don't have time for a walk," or "it's too cold, or too hot, or too late" and this robs us of the energy and desire to go for a walk. The easy drop into the old pattern takes our vitality, self-esteem, and personal power. Then guilt makes us feel bad for the choice and wears us down further. Recognizing the promptings and voice of guilt will help us break the pattern and get out for that walk. If we shift our attention away from the old dialogue to all the wonderful benefits of walking outside we will find ourselves taking a lovely walk outdoors. The walk will send messages of love to our bodies.

Breaking the pattern set in place by denial and guilt gives a real boost to our self-esteem. When we feel that boost, we should acknowledge it and stay with the vibration of how good we feel for as long as we can. It will add potency to the thought of going for a walk the next day and strengthens our healthy sense of self. It is a small step but one step at a time always takes us somewhere.

Guilt and the Perfectionist

Some of us like to think of ourselves as perfectionists. Guilt enjoys the grandiose nature of the lower ego that attempts to align with such claims. This type of perfection has no end. The truth that we are perfect, just as we are is not the song sung by the perfectionist. We cannot rest with a force driving us to attain unattainable perfection. With no rest, healing is not possible, physically, emotionally, or mentally.

Guilt and fear drive us to believe we must be perfect and must know everything. This is a road to ruin, laid by the unloving force of guilt.

Guilt finds ways to relay the messages of "it's never enough," "for things to get done right, I must do it myself," "my perfection shows I am better than most" and so on. When we listen, we make unrealistic demands of ourselves and others. The challenge is to accept ourselves completely, remain open to the light of truth, evolution, growth, and greater awareness. This path makes no unrealistic demands. This path embraces balance, healthy love of self, and the Will to grow, face our dark side, and bring it into the light where it to can evolve and empower us to experience a life filled with light, love, joy, and grace.

Guilt and Doubt

Guilt will always have us question whether we are right, good enough, and so forth. This keeps us holding back, doubting ourselves. To hold energy back rather than allow it to express is draining. Depression, poor health, and lack of personal power are some of the common outcomes from this unnatural choice. It is wise to contemplate situations but it is a trap to continuously doubt and second-guess ourselves to the point where we have no idea what information our inner guidance is attempting to share with us. When guilt continues to direct our attention to doubt, there is fear at the core of it. Self-sabotage, in its many forms, is common when we adhere to the unloving demands of guilt. If we look to the undercurrent of doubt to discover the truth, more often than not, we will find fear. When fear is expressing appropriately, it provides a guideline of protection, giving us a reason to pause and reexamine a choice. We can regain the ability to trust in our internal guidance system and ourselves. Facing our fears helps us realize that most of our fears are unfounded. This opens the free flow of energy to experience things we did not allow ourselves to experience before.

Guilt and the Loss of True Feelings

Any place within humanity that lacks acceptance is a way in for guilt. If we do not accept ourselves, we create surroundings that do not accept us. This is important to know and remember when we begin to look at what life is reflecting back. The loss of true feelings gives way to confusion, manipulations, and lost personal power. Rage is held under guilt often times because rage is deemed unacceptable by society. When rage is triggered, the expression is dramatic enough to fulfill the judgment of being unacceptable because it is out of balance. Energy is never destroyed; the transformation of all heavy energy, including rage, can evolve into understanding, acceptance, compassion, love, forgiveness, and passion. With intent to align with Source, in time, the energy will rise to meet the vibration of love. Remember the guidelines: Harm no one not even yourself.

Anytime something is held back, guilt has an opportunity to increase its presence. Anytime something is held back, everything else is affected. The longer rage is held back, the more intense the release. This is true with all old charge. The lack of balance or excessive charge is directly related to how long and how much energy has been denied and held down by guilt. When all old charge is cleared, it is not rage that will express spontaneously but anger. When anger is denied, it builds and becomes rage. When envy is denied, it builds and becomes poisonous. The more an emotion is denied, the greater the charge will be when it finally finds an outlet to express. When we habitually deny our feelings, we can become afraid of everything and nothing. Fear is typically disguised as something else. Most fear is denied rather than allowed to move and evolve into something higher. If we wait until we are triggered, the expression will likely be inappropriate in both its placement and delivery. We can consciously release safe amounts of old charge in a comfortable and safe environment by ourselves or with a trusted friend or facilitator. Life is the great reflector of our inner world. Look at your body, your relationships, how and where you live, how you spend your time and money. How do you feel about what you see? The process of seeing what we do accept and what we are not accepting is underway. Let yourself feel and, in so doing, express what has been unexpressed. As the energy moves, direct your thoughts to higher, more loving thoughts until you can naturally embrace loving, hopeful, and life-affirming thoughts.

To get current in our emotional body is a worthy goal with many rewards. Perseverance is key. Love is the force greater than the force of guilt. When we love ourselves, we can put an end to the cycle of pain and suffering. Step by step, we begin to know what our true feelings are. It is our lack of acceptance of self and our experiences that have made us blind to our divinity. It is time to wake up and expand our consciousness. This gives a way for the light of Spirit to expand and illuminate our consciousness. It frees our Will so we may regain our lost personal power, becoming courageous enough to face our fears and honor the true expression of our feelings.

Guilt and Movement

Guilt does not like movement, which is why its voice always stifles our movement, whether it is an emotion or a desire for something better. Guilt is like an invisible foot that steps on that which would bring understanding, freedom, and harmonious interaction between our Spirit and our Will. Harmony between our thoughts and our feelings will positively affect everything in our everyday lives. Inner harmony makes our ordinary days lighter, hopeful, happy, thus naturally energizing us with the vitality that is our birthright.

Guilt holds down our true feelings and silences our true voices. For guilt to be expelled, the unexpressed emotions lying underneath it must be allowed to move. This is the catalyst for change. This movement is what propels guilt out of our minds, our bodies, and our energy fields. Knowledge is power. Emotions have consciousness. We can use the knowledge we are gaining to put an end to guilt by lovingly accepting what has been denied. When we move the emotional energy that has been held down by guilt, this wave of energy will move guilt out as the emotions increase their vibratory rate and power.

Here is an example: Mary takes no steps toward developing a relationship she longs for. The voice of guilt reminds her of how little she has to offer. It tells her there is no time for such nonsense, that relationships never work out, that no one would want her. Some of Mary's true feelings repressed by guilt are fear and the feeling of being unworthy of love. If the truth was to surface, Mary would know that she really wants to love and be loved, she is afraid of getting hurt, and she would love to have someone to have fun with. She would know that she has a lot to offer. When Mary begins to allow the fear and lack of self-worth to move, her guilt sounds off saying, "What are you doing? Who do you think you are? You are just wasting your time." That is not where she should put her attention. If she began to think this through more honestly, it would sound something like this, "What am I doing? I am making room for someone to share my life with." "Who do I think I am? I am me and that is enough. I have love to give and love is meant to be shared." With attention placed on the truth, the fear rises up and has opportunity to become courage; the unworthiness rises up and has an opportunity to expand to the vibration of self-love. With the truth accepted and the emotions free, guilt has no place to be.

In another example, Ted has a fear of speaking his truth. Guilt has him believing his ideas will bring ridicule and there is no value in what he thinks. The lack of acceptance Ted has for his own right to be and be heard has been taken over by the loveless voice of guilt. He denies his true voice, and is unable to stand up for himself and represses all the emotions that go with it. With the fear of speaking the truth held in place by guilt it is easy for someone to have Ted do things he does not want to do. He is easily manipulated. How can it be different if he is not letting the people know his true feelings? He needs to feel the fear and speak the truth. Initially, it may feel like shaky ground but at least now he knows where the ground is. As he continues to speak the truth, Ted will develop a new foundation based on truthful expression. Guilt moves out on the waves of liberated fear, which can now transform into a higher vibration such as self-esteem and self-respect.

Expressing emotions we once felt too guilty to express is our gateway to freeing ourselves from the stranglehold guilt has had. Stay open for the light of new understandings that come as the energy transforms into a higher vibration. It is important to integrate the new energy by taking care of the new foundation. To do this, we quiet ourselves, care and nurture our bodies, being mindful about what is read, watched and the types of conversations we engage in. Make choices that are of a high vibration. When we love ourselves we can stabilize the new vibration rather quickly.

Know the Difference between Love and Guilt

Guilt and hatred must be moved out and the space previously held by these energies must be filled with love. A huge gap exists when we deny love in favor of guilt disguised as love. Denying love in favor of guilt can look like as benign as; "I will do this because if I don't, Jason's teacher will think I don't love him enough." The undercurrent of guilt muddies the water of the action. The foundation for doing something is no longer based on love but rather on guilt. We must come to know the difference between love and guilt. The more we choose love, free from guilt, the more things will move and shift in our inner world, which is then reflected in our outer world. The new inner peace and the new outer reflection of peace and love will be the foundation from which decisions and growth will continue.

Moving Beyond Guilt

For something new to be received, the old must go. This can be chaotic and frightening. Fear lies underneath guilt. When we move the fear, we can remove the guilt. I have allowed considerable fear to move and free itself over the years. Holding the fear or expressing irresponsibly only brought me more fear, suffering, and guilt. I did not know enough to do it responsibly and often hurt others and myself along the way. As the energy began to move, I made it about something or someone else, both directing the energy inappropriately with my thoughts and acting it out by amplifying the drama. Everyone's journey is unique unto them. There is no way to compare, yet there are similarities enough in being human that I hope you learn from my mistakes. Slowly, I learned how to allow the liberation of trapped energy the freedom to move and evolve. Sometimes it felt as if a freight train was running through my heart, shattering it into a thousand pieces, with a flood of tears washing away the rubble. Well, I say, better that than a heart attack. The beauty of this was the new landscape that began to spring forth, the new understandings, the new perspectives, and the revitalized energy with which to embrace life and come closer to knowing Source.

Though it was painful, it was liberating beyond my wildest dreams. This is a gift given to all who desire to free themselves of old charge or old baggage, as some call it. The time has come to move guilt out so God's light has room to expand illuminating, our consciousness and giving way for the Divine Mother to vibrate truthful feelings free from the heaviness brought on by guilt, judgment, and denial. What I am proposing may not be easy but living with fear ready to pounce upon us at every turn, guilt leading the way to no man's land, denial holding personal power in the dark, and judgment limiting our experiences is far more difficult. Let go and let God and the Divine Mother assist you on the road to recovery and freedom. It brings with it a sweet reward of greater awareness, more heart space available for the light of love to vibrate freely expanding truth and experiencing joy. When we walk in truth, healed and whole, we realize there is no need for any technique or medicine. In the words of Osho, "Then you live as truth – alive, radiant, contented, blissful, a song unto yourself. Your whole life becomes a prayer without any words."

Go To Bonus Media Center at:
http://www.ConsciousMastery.org/BonusMedia
To Download Bonus Media for Chapter Thirteen

New Life

CHAPTER FOURTEEN

END YOUR SUFFERING BECAUSE YOU CAN

"Be the change you want to see in the world." Mahatma Gandhi

If we believe we are all meant to suffer in order to learn then we will fulfill that belief. But if we look at that belief with the knowledge that God is loving, kind, and cares for his children, how could suffering be the only way to learn?

If we are at a point in our lives where suffering is what we are experiencing, we must remember that suffering truly means "to undergo." We are to undergo the dark aspects of our passage. We are to bring light to all that we have hidden, all that we fear, and all that we have denied and judged. There is nothing else that is asked of us. This may prove to be a tall order; however, what is reclaimed is personal power, talents, creativity, and our true deep connection with God and the Mother. All this goodness and more is willing and waiting to come home to our own heart centers, the home of the Divine within.

It is our responsibility to clear all the baggage held within our beings from the choices we have made, the experiences we have been unable to accept, the outdated belief systems we cling to, and the judgments we hold. The time is upon us. We are the ones to do this work because we can. It is within our grasp to create change that will positively affect all of life, especially children and our immediate family members. Bear in mind, we may have been carrying the seeds of dysfunction for generations. Today, we have access to so much information; making use of the knowledge of others can assist the journey of self-discovery. There is enough information to light the steps that will free our souls if we choose to make use of it. Everything we ever need to know is within us, and as such, we have within us the ability, courage, and strength to stop the long procession of passing dysfunctional, judgmental, and fearful patterns of behavior on to yet another generation.

Become Responsible for Your Growth

"Let everyone sweep in front of his own door, and the whole world will be clean." Johann Wolfgang von Goethe

Now is the time for each human being to become responsible for his or her own life including health, happiness, and overall wellness. Now is the time for us to truly know and accept that we affect everyone and everything around us by the way we act, think, and feel. Look at what we have created so far. Some of our creations are amazing and others are of such an awful nature that we do not want to admit we had anything to do with them. It is not enough to moan and groan about the atrocities in life; this communication style is counterproductive and amplifies negativity. It is enough, however, to begin with taking care of the dysfunction and suffering in our own lives, our emotional health and maturity, and our thoughts. The wellbeing of our emotional, mental, physical, and spiritual selves will have a tremendous affect not only on the lives we lead but on absolutely everything and everyone around us. If everyone took care of his or her own ground, having someone tell us what to do at every turn would be unnecessary and obsolete. We would already know deep within our hearts what constitutes a high vibrational choice, reflecting love and kindness. In this deep knowing, right action is the choice.

We truly make a difference, so let us make a positive difference. Why wait until tomorrow? When we wait for someone or something to make choices for us, we open ourselves up for suffering. Life is so much more than suffering if we allow love to flow through us. The choice to give up personal power by not making a choice keeps us weak. When we do not respond to the call of life, it is irresponsibility in action. This has never proven successful for anyone, victim or tyrant, and it never will. Anyone waiting for someone or something to save them simply needs to look within.

The guidance we long for never left us; we just forgot where to look.

Embrace a New Thought

Release the notion that we are here to suffer or that suffering is the only way. Embrace the idea that we are here to live life whole, happy, and free. Absorb the thought that we are here to enjoy life. Continue to come back to these thoughts daily until it becomes a part of life. Say aloud, "I am here to live life whole, happy, and free." We can all live abundantly, joyfully, and in harmony.

Now look upon children and imagine a world unfolding that represents the true nature of a loving Creator. Look upon children with eyes that see their innocence and open hearts that reminds us of our own innocence. It remains with us still. It may be but a small piece of its original expression but it is there nonetheless. When we rekindle the flame of our innocence, we discover a flood of trust flowing in the power of love and a loving Creator.

It will take a collective effort to change the world but that happens one individual at a time. You make a difference; we all make a difference. Nothing changes if nothing changes. Consciously doing things from a higher plane of thought will bring the change we all seek. Can we hold a vision of peace in these restless times? I say we can. Each time we realize we are beginning to spin away from peace, we must think a peaceful thought and return to the heart center.

Everything we need to evolve and heal ourselves is within us. We have inside us the strength and courage to clear ourselves and pave a better way for those who go before us, our dear elderly and for those who come after us. We suffer or have suffered, as our ancestors did, because there were not enough awakened souls to show a better way. We adopted the old patterns of suffering. The time has come to destroy that illusionary road to ruin and pave a highway to the light of truth. It all begins with one step. It all begins with you and me.

You Make a Difference

Remember, we affect everything around us, our families, our ancestors, and our planet. Would anyone bring a child into the world if they did not have the hope and desire to provide the best possible life, filled with love, joy, and happiness? Can that be done if the underlying belief is that we are sinful from the first breath and fated to suffer? We are capable of creating heaven on Earth. It is our responsibility. It is my sense that we are being asked to do this very thing. We are being given information, tools, and assistance on many levels to clear ourselves enough to make a difference for the whole of life. We can make it our personal responsibility to undergo the dark aspects of our passage with Grace and come out vibrating higher, lighter, wiser, and kinder, not only for ourselves but for the children. We do not have to get stuck in the mode of suffering, over and over. Learn what needs to be learned and the pattern ceases to exist.

We must begin with ourselves. We can see a thousand cases of people who have more challenges and dysfunctional behavior then we do to compare, judge, and blame but that is the old pattern that got us where we are now. That is not the solution. Their journeys are their own. Look to your own development. We can positively affect everything and everyone around us by the very nature of our higher vibration without having to say a word. When we do have something to say, it will be potent with love. We are already affecting everything and everyone around us but now it can be done responsibly and consciously. If we are not caring for the growing ground on which we stand, we are going to eventually walk back into the dark. Peter Marshall and many others have noted, if we do not stand for something, we will fall for anything. The nurturance of the self translates into a reality of being filled with enough light to share without exhaustion, without judgment or expectations. Light enough to speak the truth in a kind way and stand our ground because now we know where we stand. Connecting and aligning with the endless supply of love from Source makes this possible.

A Hard Look

We need to get honest with the way we have handled our lives thus far. This is not an exercise to incite more shame or regret. It is not an exercise to amplify old patterns of thought. It is an exercise for freedom from all of that and more. As a species, we are quick to accept disease and die. We seldom think twice about giving all the responsibility of our healing to someone else and rarely do we involve the healer within. We are quick to lie and to cheat ourselves out of a life of joy, health, and happiness and then share our dysfunctions with others through denial, judgment, complaining, blaming, and shaming. We are on the ready to steal from one another, even if it is energy and we cannot see it, it is still thieving. We are ready to rally against something outside ourselves but slow to bring our attention and energy inward to the war that is raging within our very being. We look outside ourselves for relief, and resist the simple act of meditation that brings peace. We are ready to accept the demands of others, even when it feels terrible, yet unwilling to accept our own needs. We will do the bidding of another, while denying the feeling within that is in opposition to the demand. Why are we so afraid to look within for the truth? Perhaps, in part, taking responsibility for our healing, our thoughts, and our feelings has not been taught to us as possible or important. Now we know that it is both possible and important. A time for change is at hand.

There exists a plethora of distractions in today's world. This makes it all the more imperative to rest within our own hearts, to commune in our own personal way with Mother/Father God, to get real with what we feel and think. It is time to discover whether or not we feel anything anymore. We should not confuse lack of feeling with mastering emotions or great strength. Our emotions can become paralyzed or frozen in time. It is time to realize it is not an asset but a detriment to our total wellness to be numb to our emotions. What do you feel and think, as you stand naked in front of a mirror? When you look at every area of your life, what do you see? All the people we encounter and the activities that make up our days have something to say about our inner reality.

The dark aspect of our passage has been avoided by all manner of distractions, pretenses, and faces. We now know that it is easier to release all the inner demons than it is to live with them. Too often we wear different faces through out the day. Are we one person at work and another one at home and still another one when with certain friends? It is time to get ourselves together and be who we are, no matter where we are or who we are with.

The extreme reflection of our troubled selves as a species is shown to us by war, greed, deceit, and violence. This is the grand scale reflection of what is going on within humanity. We must check the undercurrents that exist in our own beings. You are the only one who can truly know what lies under the surface in you. Here is an easy test to let you know if you have any shadows hiding within: are you glowing with visible white or golden light? No? Ha! Then a part of you is still in the dark. Looks like we all have some work to do.

When we spend time in nature, we discover not all the work of transforming our energy is painful and difficult. Nature provides a great place to move energy and inspires a playfulness that is essential to our wholeness. Expressing creatively in any form is another playful and positively effective way to move and clear repressed energy.

A belief in suffering is one of the core causes for suffering and disease. If we are determined to be free of suffering, we will be free. Look inward to discover the cause of your own suffering. Break the pattern on your core cause for suffering and clear the vessel that you are. Feel what needs to be felt and free yourself of the inner demons or shadows that make suffering part of your reality. Divine assistance is only a request away. Ask for help and it will come. Stay open for whatever way it presents itself; it may surprise you.

What Will It Take?

What will it take for us, as a species, to wake up, embrace the responsibility of life and clear our shadows? What will it take for you? Your individual work to clear yourself is vital. You are so important and so valuable that God and the Mother have given you everything you need to evolve if you accept it. If you are fearful of change then move the fear and discover what the fear actually is. More often than not there is little to no substance in the fear. Its only power to control you comes from your refusal to look at it up close and personal. The counsel written over the gateway to the temple at Delphi was "Know Thyself." Consider that with intent to understand and you will find yourself traveling on thought waves you never knew existed. It is time to come together within ourselves and then gather with others who generously and fearlessly shine their light. The more we get to know our true selves, the more we will love all that we are.

Do You Feel Trapped?

When we continue to say we have no choice, that we have to do this or must do that, then we are investing energy in our limitations. If we do that, much of our power goes to support and prove those limitations. We suffer when we resist the flow of love and see situations for our growth as obstacles. We trap ourselves in the cycle of suffering when we deny our true power of choice. When we deny our divinity, we deny the very nature of who we are and have always been. Denial has us investing energy in believing we are so much less. Transforming outdated beliefs, patterns of behavior, and repressed energy is possible with recognition and acceptance. Without it, a cycle of suffering becomes our lot in life. To undergo our journey with Grace brings suffering to an end. This requires our attention and acceptance of what is, coupled with true intent and desire to experience a life of happiness and the belief that we are worthy of such a life. We must become responsible for all that our lives are presenting. Participation in the conscious creation of our lives is vital.

Parents and Children

Children are masters at feeling the undercurrents from others. When they do, they typically feel emotions they cannot understand and may even deny. If they ask candid questions, it is your responsibility to answer them honestly with sensitivity and provide an environment that allows them to feel safe enough to express themselves honestly. If what they feel and what we say does not match up, they become confused. When denial begins to erode their innocence they will suffer.

Excuses

We often have excuses or reasons why we cannot take responsibility for ourselves. We rely on those excuses to pave the road for our days and years to come because we believe our excuse to be true. When we travel deeper into any of the excuses that color our lives, we will come to see many of our own shadows.

It does not matter how logical the excuses may seem, how desperately we want to defend them or how well accepted or sculpted they are, an excuse is still an excuse. If the presence of disease excuses us from participating in life, we can still choose to participate in our healing process along with the chosen physician. This shifts the energy from an excuse to embracing personal power and the inner healer. Thoughts of connecting with the body and adding healing, loving energy to the wound or disease will open a great gateway of love and transformation. Disease is not an excuse; it is a reason to get involved in life on a deeper level. The quality of life depends on it. When the choice is made to consciously dive into the disease, it brings light enough to discover the cause. It brings energy and conscious involvement of our inner healer and the real possibility of self-healing.

If our excuse is time, then we are slaves to our own minds and the outside world at large. When our thoughts and our feelings are not aligned our spirit pushes us to hard. We have lost touch and do not feel when it is time to rest, balance, get quiet, and care for ourselves as a whole being. Recognizing excuses for what they are provides a great starting point where freedom can begin. Dive into the belief you have no time and see how you really spend it. Do you have to get a cold or get sick before you stop and rest? Do you waste time in front of the TV, reading gossip, talking gossip, and other life denying activities, all of which sap energy? All of these examples are expenditures of time. Track your spending.

Excuses are like arrows, pointing us in the direction that needs our attention. If we choose to dive in and take a deeper look, we will free ourselves from the endless cycle of imbalance and suffering. Suffering need not be a disease or poverty. It can be as seemingly benign as not having enough resources such as time, energy, and money to enjoy life. From the perspective of a whole being embracing the consciousness of lack as a reality is suffering. It reflects a lack of balance, which is vital to the wellness of our total selves. We do not have to die to receive the blessings of health, joy, and love in the afterlife. We can experience heaven on Earth. When our inner world and our outer reality are one and the same, reflecting kindness, joy, and love, we have truly taken a stand for life, for light and for heaven on Earth.

Shine Your Light

Make self-honesty the driving force of your divine power and it will not disappoint you. You need not make a great stand openly in the world, but you do need to take a responsible stand in your own life. Ignite the fire within and acknowledge your own divinity. It is you that must nurture that tiny spark until it ignites your Spirit. It will shine light on much of what you fear. It will shine light on your beliefs, conscious and unconscious, that are not in alignment with the truth, love, and Source. This will help you know what to let go of. It will shed light on your talents and strengths so that you can now begin to nurture and cultivate them. When you get ignition, maintain the flame by caring for your growing ground. Your growing ground is your expanding consciousness, new perspectives, and renewed energy. When your flame is well maintained and well nurtured, it will grow bigger. You will know when the time is right for you to gather with others and you will recognize the flame of love and desire that burns in the hearts of like-minded and like-vibrational beings. Right time, right place, and right action accompany us on our journey when our inner light is turned on and shining brightly. We will flow to one another effortlessly.

Likewise, there will be those who flow away from us. Let them go with nothing but your blessing. In the pain of separation and change, you must feel all the feelings that rise up but you must be responsible for them. Your thoughts move through matter and have a way of uplifting or tearing down the energy of others and yourself. Do not allow angry curses to fly with a particular target in mind. You will cause harm to others and to yourself. Move your emotions as befitting the being of light that you are. When your own energy is strong, flowing, and connected with Source, you would not even consider taking energy from another or harming another in any way. Being given the tools and the choice to use them prepares you for creating the best life ever.

We Are Not Alone

Remember, we are not alone in this. Source is but a heartbeat away. If we make room in our hearts for the presence of the Divine to grow, we will be shown the way. When we call for the energy of Grace to assist our passage we rise up with the understanding that love sets us on a new foundation of living heaven on Earth. We are returning to our innocence and our magnificence. Grow in the ability to embrace your divinity and the light will surely illuminate your path.

"You are not only responsible for what you say, but also for what you do not say." Martin Luther

Go To Bonus Media Center at:
http://www.ConsciousMastery.org/BonusMedia
To Download Bonus Media for Chapter Fourteen

AFTERWORD

Be You

The truth can be painful but it never fails to liberate. With liberation comes a whole new vista and way of living life that supports who we truly are. We are all one, yet through the beauty of differentiation, we are all uniquely different. It is wise to come to know ourselves, to embrace the special beings that we are. The time is at hand to understand our important contribution to the whole of life.

How does it feel to be you? Happiness is contagious. Let it bubble up, feel it, become it, spread it around, and surround yourself with happy people. Trust yourself.

When we trust in who we are, we are able to appreciate our differences, to give room to others to express their own unique blend of energy, knowing that we all have a right to be here. When we respect ourselves, we can respect others; when we accept ourselves, we can accept others. We begin to see our differences as a beautiful tapestry, rather than something to fear or destroy. There is nothing to fear in our differences. It is the marvel of creation, finding expression through humans, plants, animals, crystals, and all that we share this planet with. We are all beautiful children of this universe *sharing* the planet, the beautiful Mother Earth. Let's get ourselves together and remember: The power to create heaven on Earth is within us, individually and collectively. As we discover our true selves we will find heaven within and lovingly allow Heaven on Earth to be the reflection we see in our outer reality.

Enter the chamber of your heart. Everything you need to heal and evolve is there waiting for you to accept it. Turn on your light. See for yourself.

Unless you turn and become like children, you will never enter the kingdom of heaven – Jesus

Personal Road Map

Our lives, when viewed honestly, are road maps of all we hold near and dear and all we deny and fear. When we become observers of our own lives and of the choices we have made, we can take the next step of accepting what we have created thus far. When we let more of the truth unfold, we can see the decisions we have made without judging ourselves. Inner listening is an important part of the process of our growth. This is difficult, if not impossible, if our minds are filled with distractions and inner conflict clamoring for our attention. It is wise to bear in mind that to make no decision is a decision. We have simply abdicated the power to decide to someone or something else. This road map of our lives will show us the pathways that bring truthful feelings into our thought processes. The truth does set us free and will be our guiding light, pointing to choices that reflect the divine beings that we are. Truthful feelings are our souls' contributions; inspired thought and action are the contributions of our spirits. When both are free we are happy, healthy, and beautifully aligned with Source.

CONCLUSION

We all have a desire to live our lives to the fullest with great joy, abundance, and heartfelt appreciation. This seed was planted long ago and is our birthright. It is natural for us to desire to grow, experience more, share, learn, and be more than we have allowed ourselves to be so far. As the seed breaks open, revealing new growth, there is a tenderness that will require us take great care of ourselves and be courageous in the face of the new life unfolding.

Conscious Mastery will help you understand how old patterns of behavior and the same unwanted experiences return. When we begin to see and recognize how energy is working in our lives, we can begin to make changes, large and small, that resonate with the life we desire and deserve. A chapter is devoted to the many ways you can release energy in a conscious and safe way. When we let go of all that holds us back and holds us down, we create space for a new and better way to experience life on Earth. Your desire for a better life is the beginning of creating a better life.

When we walk through our confusion, we will find clarity.
When we walk through our fear, we will discover our courage.
When we walk through our grief, we will find joy.
When we walk through our anger, we will find peace.

Everything we can walk through, we can transform. When we feel honest feelings and acknowledge our thoughts with the intent to align with love, we are walking into a life of our choosing. We are walking out of the dark and into the light.

Astara Teal Summers

ABOUT THE AUTHOR

Astara Teal Summers is Chief Visionary Officer of ConsciousMastery.org and OrignialSparkMusic.com and the author of *Expand With Love*. Astara's inspirational blog and e-books are loved by readers throughout the world. Astara is a troubadour whose time has come to spread the message of love, hope, and peace to the world through her music, art, and writing. After surviving a tragic motorcycle accident, the love and healing that flowed through her came in the form of songs. The music in time gave birth to the teachings, writings, and the principles of Conscious Mastery®. Her connection with nature has always been strong, finding both peace and inspiration communing with Mother Earth.

Six thousand year old Vedic writings and songs explain the name Astara as "the place where the rays of light shine from behind to light the pathway ahead."

Today, Astara facilitates Conscious Mastery® group classes where participants explore meditation, journal writing, art, music and sound and body movement creating an opening for them to better understand themselves and their lives. She also offers private sessions for adults and teens.

Born in Eau Claire, Wisconsin, Astara has enjoyed living on both US coasts, in the red rock canyons of Sedona, on the secret beaches of Kauai, and in the mountains of Colorado. She currently resides in Tallahassee, Florida with her husband and son.

REFERENCES/RESOURCES

Many books provided new perspectives while others offered validation. In some way they all provided an opportunity to grow, feel, and think for myself.

Bible
Bhagavad - Gita As It Is
Illusions - Richard Bach
Johnathan Livingston Seagull - Richard Bach
The Essential Rumi - Translated by Coleman Banks with John Moyne
Matrix Energetic - Richard Bartlett DC ND
The Physics of Miracles - Richard Bartlett DC ND
The Secret Music of the Soul - Patrick Bernhardt
Ageless body timeless mind- Deepak Chopra
The Path of Love - Deepak Chopra
The Seven Spiritual Laws of Success - Deepak Chopra
The Spontaneous fulfillment of Desire - Deepak Chopra
The Way of the Wizard - Deepak Chopra
The Alchemist - Paulo Coelho
Original Cause - Ceanne DeRohan
Right Use of Will - Ceanne DeRohan
Women who run with the Wolves - Clarissa Pinkola Estes
The Prophet - Kahlil Gibran
The Voice of the Master - Kahlil Gibran
Power vs. Force - David Hawkins MD PhD
Heal Your Body - Louise Hay

Siddhartha - Herman Hess
Ask and It Is Given - Ester and Jerry Hicks Teachings of Abraham
The Astonishing Power of Emotions - Ester and Jerry Hicks Teachings of Abraham
Chakra Balancing - Anodea Judith
Ramtha-The White Book - JZ King
The Secret History of Consciousness - Meg Blackburn Losey PhD
The Ancient Secret of the Flower of Life Vol. 1 - Drunvalo Melchizedek
Sacred Journey of the Peaceful Warrior - Dan Millman
The Peaceful Warrior - Dan Millman
The Heroine's Journey - Maureen Murdock
The Power of Positive Thinking - Dr. Norman Vincent Peale
Creative Abundance - Elizabeth Clare Prophet
Violet Flame to Heal Body Mind and Soul - Elizabeth Clare Prophet
Celestine Prophesy - James Redfield
Soul Love - Sanaya Roman
The Four Agreements - Miguel Ruiz
The Book of Chakra Healing - Liz Simpson
Voices of the Earth - Scott Silverston
An Ascension Handbook -Tony Stubbs
What is Lightbody? - Tashira Tachi-ren
The Power of I Am - John Maxwell Taylor
Grace, Gaia and the End of Days - Stuart Wilde
Silent Power - Stuart Wilde
Autobiography of a Yogi - Paramahansa Yogananda

Self-Realization Fellowship http://www.yogananda-srf.org